Classic
Motorbikes

This is a Parragon Book
First published in 2007

Parragon
Queen Street House
4 Queen Street
Bath BA1 1HE, UK

Copyright © Parragon Books Ltd 2007

Designed, produced and packaged by Stonecastle Graphics Ltd

Text by Roland Brown
Designed by Sue Pressley and Paul Turner
Edited by Anthony John

ISBN 978-1-4054-8661-3

Printed in China

Photographic credits

Mac McDiarmid: page 28
Andrew Morland: pages 11 right, 14, 15, 21, 25, 30, 31
Garry Stuart: pages 12, 13, 16, 17, 19, 20, 26, 27, 29,
   35 below, 62, 88, 110, 172
Gold & Goose: page 166

Roland Brown library/www.motobike.net
   (fees to Riders for Health); photos by:
BMW: pages 22 top, 23, 155, 168, 188 below
Honda: pages 160, 178, 181
Yamaha: pages 132, 176

Photos © Roland Brown library/www.motobike.net by:
Kevin Ash: page 117
Roland Brown: pages 6, 7, 10, 11 left, 22 below, 67, 77,
   93, 99, 100, 103, 106, 107, 120, 121 top, 133, 135,
   137 left, 139, 140, 141, 144, 145, 146 right, 147, 151,
   157, 164, 165, 167, 180 top, 188 top
Jack Burnicle: pages 104-5, 124, 125, 127, 142 left, 148
Phil Masters: pages 18, 24, 36, 37, 38-9, 40, 41, 42, 44,
   45, 47, 48, 49, 52, 54, 56, 57, 61, 63, 64, 65, 66, 68,
   69, 73, 74-5, 80, 81, 82, 83, 84, 85, 86, 87, 90, 91, 92,
   94, 95, 96, 97, 111, 114, 115, 116, 119, 122, 123,
   126, 131, 138, 142 right, 146 left, 149, 152-3, 156,
   158, 159, 163, 169, 170 173, 174, 175, 179, 180 below,
   182, 184, 185, 189
Gold & Goose: pages 1, 76, 89, 118, 183, 186, 187,
   190, 191
Mac McDiarmid: pages 112, 161
Oli Tennent: pages 3, 8-9, 32, 33, 34, 35t, 43, 46, 50, 51,
   53, 55, 58, 59, 60, 70, 71, 72, 78, 79, 101, 102, 108,
   109, 113, 121 below, 128, 129, 130, 134, 136, 137
   right, 143, 150, 154, 162, 171, 177

Classic
Motorbikes
THE WORLD'S GREATEST MODELS

Roland Brown

Bath · New York · Singapore · Hong Kong · Cologne · Delhi · Melbourne

Contents

Introduction	6

Chapter 1 **Pre-War Classics** 8

FN Four	10
Pierce Four	12
Pope V-twin	13
Zenith Gradua	14
Harley-Davidson Model 11F	15
Flying Merkel	16
Cyclone	17
Douglas 2.75hp	18
Indian Powerplus	19
Excelsior Super X	20
BSA Model E	21
BMW R32	22
Ner-A-Car	24
Norton CS1	25
Henderson Model KJ	26
Indian Scout	27
Rudge Ulster	28
Crocker	29
Excelsior Manxman	30
Harley-Davidson Model 61E	31
Brough Superior	32
Norton Big Four	34
Indian Four	35
Triumph Speed Twin	36

Chapter 2 **Post-War Classics** 38

Ariel Square Four	40
Scott Flying Squirrel	42
Sunbeam S7 De Luxe	43
Vincent Rapide	44
Harley-Davidson WL45	46
Gilera Saturno	47
Moto Guzzi Airone	48
Norton Model 7	49
Indian Chief	50
AJS Model 16MCS	52
Moto Rumi 125 Sport	53
Triumph Tiger 100	54
Velocette MAC	55
Douglas Dragonfly	56
Ariel Red Hunter	57
BSA Gold Star DBD34 Clubman	58
Sunbeam S8	60
BSA Road Rocket	61
Harley-Davidson Sportster	62
Velocette LE	63
Triumph Thunderbird 650	64
Royal Enfield Constellation	66
Harley-Davidson Duo-Glide	67
Norton Dominator 88	68
Honda C71	69
BSA A10 Golden Flash	70
Matchless G12	71
Triumph TR6 Trophy	72
Panther Model 100	73

Chapter 3 **The 1960s** 74

Honda CB92	76
Moto Guzzi Falcone	77
Triumph T120 Bonneville	78
Norton 650SS Dominator	80
Ariel Leader	81
Honda CB72	82
BSA Rocket Gold Star	83
Yamaha YDS-2	84
BMW R69S	86
Royal Enfield Continental GT	87
Harley-Davidson Electra Glide	88
Honda CB450	89
Dresda Triton	90
Velocette Venom Thruxton	92
Suzuki T20 Super Six	93
Kawasaki 250SG	94
Bridgestone 350 GTR	95
Suzuki T500	96
BSA Spitfire MkIV	97
Norton Commando	98
Kawasaki W2TT Commander	100
Triumph T150 Trident	101
Moto Guzzi V7 Special	102
Yamaha XS-1	103

Chapter 4 **The 1970s** 104

Honda CB750	106	Yamaha XT500	132
Yamaha YR-5	108	Suzuki GT550	133
Norton Commando 750S	109	Laverda Jota	134
Harley-Davidson FX Super Glide	110	Yamaha RD400C	135
BSA Lightning 650	111	Moto Guzzi Le Mans 850	136
Laverda 750 SFC	112	Triumph T140 Bonneville Silver Jubilee	138
Kawasaki H2 750	113	Suzuki GS750	139
Suzuki GT750	114	Harley-Davidson XLCR1000 Café Racer	140
BMW R75/5	116	Yamaha XS750	141
Moto Guzzi V7 Sport	117	Bimota SB2	142
Triumph X-75 Hurricane	118	MV Agusta 850 Magni	143
Ducati 350 Scrambler	119	Quasar	144
Kawasaki Z1	120	Suzuki GS1000	145
MV Agusta 750 Sport	122	Honda CBX1000	146
BMW R90S	123	Yamaha XS1100	148
Benelli 750 Sei	124	Ducati Darmah SD	149
Triumph T160 Trident	125	Honda CB900F	150
Suzuki RE-5	126	Kawasaki Z1300	151
Ducati 900SS	127		
Honda GL1000 Gold Wing	128		
Honda CB400F	130		
Bultaco Metralla 250 GTS	131		

Chapter 5 **The 1980s** 152

Suzuki GSX1100	154
BMW R80 G/S	155
Moto Guzzi V1000 Convert	156
Kawasaki GPz1100	157
Yamaha RD350LC	158
Honda CB1100R	160
Hesketh V1000	161
Ducati Pantah	162
Laverda Montjuic Mk2	163
Honda CX500 Turbo	164
Suzuki GSX1100S Katana	166
Kawasaki Z1100R	167
BMW K100RS	168
Yamaha RD500LC	169
Honda VF1000R	170
Kawasaki GPZ900R	171
Harley-Davidson FXST Softail	172
Yamaha V-Max	173
Suzuki GSX-R750	174
Yamaha FZ750	176
Bimota DB1	177
Honda VFR750F	178
Suzuki GSX-R1100	179
Yamaha FJ1200	180
Honda CBR600F	181
Norton Classic	182
Harley-Davidson XLH1200 Sportster	183
Honda RC30	184
Bimota YB8	186
Buell RS1200	187
BMW K1	188
Kawasaki ZXR750	189
Ducati 851	190

Index 192

Introduction

The interest in classic motorcycles seems to grow with every passing year, as demonstrated by the huge variety of club runs, shows, races, auctions and other events taking place around the world. It's only natural for motorcyclists to admire the great machines of the past; those that were owned and cherished, or maybe just dreamed about, years ago, especially when many of these old bikes don't just look good, but are also great fun to ride.

In many cases they're also inexpensive to buy and run. Many enthusiasts still yearn for an immaculate Brough Superior or Ducati 750SS, but less exotic classics are much in demand too. While new models have been getting more powerful and sophisticated in recent years, a more important benefit to many motorcyclists has been the growing availability of older machines that are rideable, reliable and relatively cheap.

The precise nature of a classic bike has long been the subject of heated debate. Some machines built as recently as the 1980s generate as much nostalgia as an immaculate Indian Chief or BSA Gold Star does to an older generation. Many riders' formative motorcycling years were in the 1970s, when Japanese superbikes arrived, and glamorous Italian sportsters provided a thrilling alternative. Plenty of

Below: The world's first production motorcycle was the 1489cc Hildebrand & Wolfmüller, built in Germany for four years from 1894. The four-stroke parallel twin's cylinders lay horizontally. Maximum power output was 2.5hp, giving a top speed of almost 30mph (48km/h).

Opposite below: The progress in early motorcycle design is shown by two US-produced bikes: the steam-driven Geneva (left) from 1896; and the Thomas, which followed four years later with a 1.8hp petrol engine in its bicycle style frame.

other riders still affectionately recall the 1960s and earlier, when British bikes ruled the roads and Harley-Davidson, BMW and others joined in with their own distinctive machines.

From time to time people attempt to define a classic bike, in the way that veteran motorcycles are officially those built before 1915, and vintage covers those produced between 1915 and 1930. But it's rare that agreement is reached. Many very old bikes undoubtedly qualify, but a description or cut-off year is infinitely harder to pin down.

One dictionary definition of classic is 'of outstanding quality', and the machines selected for this book certainly fall into that category. Each is special in its own way; from Harley-Davidson's sophisticated 1915-model V-twin to Triumph's legendary Bonneville; from Honda's revolutionary CB750 four to Moto Guzzi's popular 250cc Airone. Together they show how the motorcycle has changed dramatically while its essential appeal has stayed much the same.

There are striking similarities between many machines of different eras. This book's first entry, FN's Four of more than a century ago, and the last, Ducati's 1989-model 851, share features ranging from a twistgrip throttle on the handlebars to the engine's location between the rider's shins. Between those two bikes are many unique, brilliant and very different machines. Whether with performance, technical innovation, commercial success or simply style, each played a part in bringing motorcycling to where it is today.

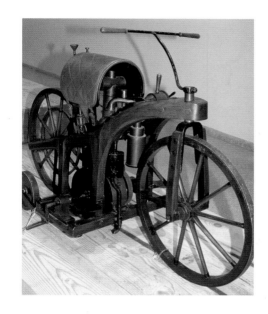

Above: The very first motorcycle was German engineer Gottlieb Daimler's 'Einspur' or 'One-track', a 264cc device with a wooden frame. It was ridden for roughly eight miles (13km) by Daimler's son Paul in 1885.

Chapter 1

Pre-War Classics

FN Four

Belgian firm FN's Four was one of the most successful machines of motorcycling's early years, as well as one of the most sophisticated. By no means everyone had been convinced by the relatively complex Four on its unveiling in 1904. French publication *France Automobile*'s reviewer commented that: 'It has a remarkable engine; however, we regard it more as a curiosity than a practical motor cycle'. But the Four would remain in production, through several redesigns, until 1926.

Its appeal was easy to understand. As well as the eye-catching four-cylinder engine that gave the bike its name, the Four incorporated advanced design features including telescopic forks and shaft final drive. Its smoothness and reliability gave it an advantage over most rival machines.

The FN initials were a shortening of Fabrique Nationale d'Armes de Guerre. The company from Herstal, near Liège, had been set up in 1899 to produce

Below: The FN Four was a well-produced machine with a tubular-steel frame, wide handlebars, efficient mudguards, bicycle-style saddle and, in the case of this immaculately restored example, a headlight plus a speedometer driven by the front wheel.

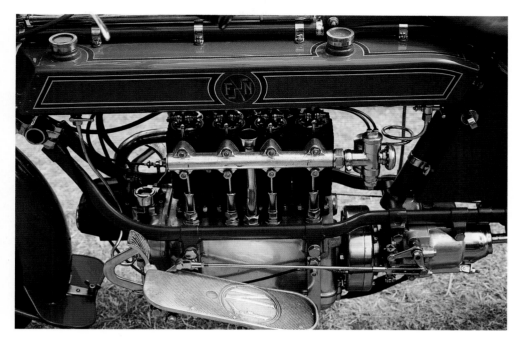

Above: This Four's list of sophisticated features included footboards as well as the shaft final drive that was fitted to all but the last models.

Above left: The FN's engine size varied over the years. By the time this bike was built for the US market in 1908, capacity had increased from the original 362cc to 498cc.

armaments. Bicycles had been added two years later, and in 1902 FN built its first motorcycles, using 225cc and 286cc single-cylinder engines. Those early singles prompted FN to attempt a more ambitious model, and to design it the company turned to Paul Kelecom, who had gained experience by designing and building engines under his own name. Kelecom's motors had been used by Ormonde, a London-based firm that had adopted one to compete in the prestigious Paris-Madrid marathon in 1903.

In an attempt to avoid the problems encountered in the Paris-Madrid, notably vibration and slipping drive belts, Kelecom set to work on a four-cylinder engine with shaft drive. The resultant 362cc powerplant's smoothness allowed it to be mounted in a relatively light, twin-loop frame. Other chassis details were thoughtfully designed, notably the telescopic front suspension system, which combined with a parallelogram linkage. No rear suspension or front brake were provided. Instead the FN featured two rear brakes: a drum that was operated by the rider pedalling backwards, and a hand-operated contracting band that worked on the outside of the drum.

That engine was the FN's main attraction. Valve layout was typical of the time, with cam-operated exhaust valves plus 'automatic' inlet valves – ie opened by piston suction alone, and closed by a light spring. Bottom-end design featured a long, one-piece crankshaft in a cast-iron crankcase whose four small mica windows allowed the rider to check that oil was reaching the main bearings.

Performance was smooth rather than spectacular, but by 1911 the Four's capacity had increased via 412cc to 491cc, giving a slightly increased top speed of about 40mph (64km/h). Another update raised capacity to 748cc just before World War I, during which the occupied FN factory at Herstal was used to build bikes for the Germany army.

Following the end of the War the Four's appeal faded. It was redesigned once again in 1923, this time gaining a chain final drive in place of the shaft. The Belgian firm finally ended its production three years later, but the classy Four had proved all its doubters wrong long before that.

FN Four (1906)	
Engine Air-cooled inlet-over-exhaust eight-valve in-line four	
Capacity 412cc (48 x 57mm)	
Maximum power 4bhp	
Transmission Single speed, shaft final drive	
Frame Steel twin downtube	
Suspension Telescopic front; rigid rear	
Brakes None front; drum and contracting band rear	
Weight 165lb (75kg) dry	
Top speed 40mph (64km/h)	

Pierce Four

The Pierce family of Buffalo, New York, was well known for bicycles and its glamorous Pierce-Arrow automobiles when Percy, son of founder George, set up the Pierce Cycle Company. Percy aimed to create a suitably upmarket two-wheeler, taking inspiration from the Belgian-built four-cylinder FN with which he had returned from a trip to Europe. His firm's debut machine became the first American-built four when it entered production in 1909.

FN's influence was clear in the Pierce's design, but the new bike was not a copy. Its larger, 696cc (43ci) engine was a side-valve design, complete with FN-style shaft drive. It produced about 4bhp. Sections of the frame were built from large-diameter steel tubes which also held fuel and oil. Quality of both workmanship and materials was outstandingly high, in keeping with the Pierce-Arrow reputation. The bike was advertised as the 'Pierce Vibrationless Motorcycle'; a machine that would 'give motorcar comfort, and travel comfortably from a mere walking pace up to the speed of the motorcar'.

The Four was certainly both smooth and fast, with a top speed of over 50mph (81km/h). It was also reliable enough to win several endurance events. Inevitably it was also expensive, with a price of $350 that made it the most costly machine on the US market in 1910. Unfortunately for Pierce, it was not profitable even at that price. An estimated 3500 of the sophisticated Fours had been sold by 1913, when the bankrupt Pierce Cycle Company built its last machine.

Above: The Pierce's cleverly engineered chassis used the large-diameter frame to hold fuel, and employed the final drive shaft as a structural component.

Above: The Pierce's smooth-running 696cc in-line four-cylinder engine used a side-valve layout to produce a maximum of 4bhp.

Pope V-twin

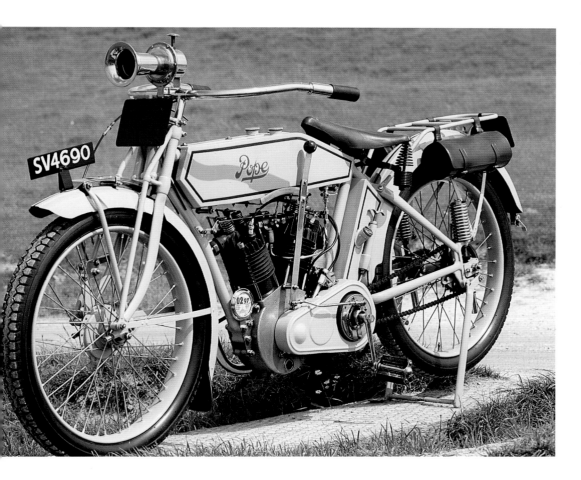

Above: *Pope's powerful overhead-valve V-twin provided excellent performance when the bike was launched in 1912.*

Left: *The Model L's chassis incorporated leaf-spring front suspension, a plunger-style rear system, and a two-speed gearbox operated by a lever to the left of the tank.*

Massachusetts firm Pope built its reputation on sophisticated bikes featuring overhead-valve V-twin engines, plus suspension at both front and rear. Albert Pope was a former civil war soldier who built bicycles and cars before producing his first motorcycle, a humble 500cc single, in 1911. Just a year later he uprated the single with pushrod-operated overhead valve gear, and doubled up the cylinders to create a powerful 1000cc V-twin.

The V-twin made an immediate impact, not least because there was no overhead-valve rival on the US market. Pope's production machines produced about 12bhp, and rapidly proved highly competitive in local race meetings. In 1913, Pope riders scored significant wins against Excelsior and Indian. But disappointment followed when Pope put together a works team for the following season's big races. The overhead-cam valve gear proved a liability as problems eliminated the Popes from long-distance events at Dodge City and Venice in California.

Those racing problems did not prevent Pope's roadster from being impressively quick and capable. In standard form the V-twin was good for over 60mph (97km/h), and its sophisticated features included two-speed transmission. The chassis combined leaf-spring front suspension with a version of the plunger type rear suspension that would be used by other manufacturers in the 1930s. But Pope lacked the investment to compete with its larger rivals. By the end of the decade, Albert Pope's motorcycle venture had come to an end.

Pope V-twin (1914)	
Engine	Air-cooled ohv pushrod four-valve V-twin
Capacity	999cc (84.5 x 89mm)
Maximum power	12bhp
Transmission	Three-speed, chain final drive
Frame	Steel single downtube
Suspension	Leaf spring front, plunger rear
Brakes	None front, drum rear
Weight	305lb (138kg)
Top speed	70mph (113km/h)

Zenith Gradua

Zenith motorcycles will long be remembered for the Gradua gear system, which was revolutionary when invented by the Surrey firm's designer Freddie Barnes in 1908. Until that time, the only way that the rider of a typical belt-drive motorcycle could adjust the machine's gearing was to alter the position of the crankshaft pulley that took drive from the engine to the rear wheel. This system's flaw was that if belt tension was correct in high gear, it was too slack in low gear.

Barnes' Gradua system got round that problem using a long handle, nicknamed the 'coffee grinder', which ran up the right side of the engine and was connected at its bottom to both the crankshaft pulley and the rear wheel. When the coffee-grinder was turned, it moved both the pulley and rear wheel spindle, maintaining drive-belt tension while the gearing was changed.

The Gradua was successfully fitted to various engines. Barnes himself rode a Zenith fitted with the device to win 53 hill climbs in 1911 alone, outclassing its single-speed rivals to such a degree that the organising Auto-Cycle Union barred the Gradua from entering further events.

Zenith utilised this ban to advertise their bikes, most memorably by introducing a badge that featured the word 'Barred' and pictured a motorcycle behind the bars of a jail. Zenith continued to use the logo long after the Gradua had been superseded by Rudge's Multi system. The firm eventually closed down in 1930, although small numbers were built by a London dealer into the 1940s.

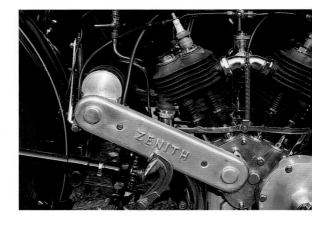

Above: This 1914-model Zenith's 550cc JAP engine was one of many to benefit from the Gradua gear system.

Below: The Gradua's angled 'coffee-grinder' lever is visible above the petrol tank. The system would have helped this V-twin to carry the extra weight of a sidecar.

Harley-Davidson Model 11F

arley-Davidson's Model 11F was not the only V-twin to make its mark for the Milwaukee factory in 1915. As well as the handsome and successful 989cc roadster, Harley built a tuned and lightened version called the Model 11K that brought the firm its first big racing success when rider Otto Walker won two prestigious long-distance events against factory opposition.

But it was the Model 11F roadster on which Harley's commercial success depended, and the 10bhp machine proved well up to the job. Six years after the Model D, the firm's first V-twin, had proved an unreliable disaster, the Model 11 showed that chief engineer William Harley and his three co-founders, the Davidson brothers, had learned much from that disappointment.

The 11F's V-twin engine kept the 45-degree cylinder angle that Harley had used all along, with inlet-over-exhaust valve layout, but it was a much improved machine. Its key features, some of which had been introduced over the previous few years, included a new frame with lower seat and sprung 'Ful Floteing' seatpost, plus footboards, enclosed valve springs, kick-starter, a more sophisticated lubrication system, and two-speed transmission with optional chain instead of belt final drive.

The Model 11F had a top speed of 60mph (97km/h), handled well with the help of girder fork front suspension, and enhanced Harley's reputation for strength and reliability. Its basic design would be retained, through numerous updates, for another 15 years as the Milwaukee firm confirmed its status as one of America's leading manufacturers.

Above: *The Model 11F featured the grey paintwork of many early Harleys but was a much more sophisticated bike than the firm's first V-twin of 1909.*

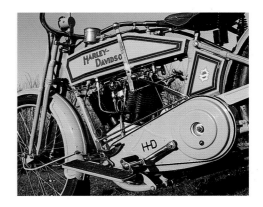

Above: *Harley's 45-degree degree V-twin gained a three-speed gearbox in 1915, but starting remained by pedal until a kickstarter was introduced for the following year.*

Flying Merkel

The powerful bikes built by Joseph Merkel's firm justified the advertising line: 'If it passes you, it's a Flying Merkel'. Famous racer Maldwyn Jones was one of several riders who were successful on the striking, orange-painted Flying Merkels, although the company often found selling bikes more difficult than winning races.

Many of Merkel's machines were innovative as well as fast. After starting with single-cylinder bikes and moving his firm from Milwaukee to Pennsylvania in 1909, he invented a compact sprung front fork unit and a cantilever rear suspension system that was similar to that later used by Vincent. The next year he adopted the Flying Merkel name, and used it for a big 1000cc V-twin.

In 1911 the firm was bought by the Miami Cycle Company, and production moved to Ohio. Joe Merkel continued to innovate, introducing features including mechanical intake valves, and a combined oil tank and seat post. Race ace Jones also helped development, notably in designing some low, braced handlebars that helped him win more than half of the events he entered between 1913 and 1915.

But the bikes' speed and Jones' skill could not keep Flying Merkel in business. Joe Merkel had left in 1913, and the firm was hit by huge servicing and legal costs when the spring-powered self-starter fitted to its touring bikes proved unreliable. By the end of 1915 the American motorcycle market's contraction, partly due to the arrival of Ford's Model T car, had resulted in Flying Merkel production coming to an end.

Above: *Joe Merkel's V-twins attracted attention with their orange paintwork and Flying Merkel name as well as their speed, but often suffered from unreliability.*

Below: *This Flying Merkel dates from 1910 and is a pure-bred racer that would have lapped a board track at high speed without either suspension or brakes.*

Cyclone

Above: Its overhead camshafts with bevel-shaft drive helped make Cyclone's 45-degree V-twin engine one of the most powerful and sophisticated of its day.

Above left: This 1915-model roadster combines Cyclone's yellow paintwork with left-spring front suspension, sprung saddle and a drum rear brake.

yclone's powerful and technically advanced V-twins were among the fastest and most spectacular bikes of their day, but not the most commercially successful. The Cyclone brand was launched in 1913 by the Joerns Motor Manufacturing Company, based in St Paul, Minnesota. Its machines were powered by 996cc V-twin engines with cylinders set at 45 degrees, and with the rarity of overhead camshafts, driven by bevel shaft.

Designer Andrew Stroud's powerplant was notable for its impressive power output – figures quoted range from 25bhp for the roadsters to 45bhp for the factory racebikes – and for its state-of-the-art engineering, which included lightweight conrods and a roller-bearing crankshaft. The chassis featured a steel frame that held the fuel tank between its horizontal top tubes, and cradled the engine in its U-shaped lower section. Most roadster models had leaf-spring suspension at both front and rear. Racebikes were generally unsprung and had distinctive yellow paintwork.

The Cyclones' speed and technology meant that they created quite a stir, boosted by the spectacular efforts of factory racer Don Johns. More publicity came when development engineer J A McNeil lapped the board track at Omaha, Nebraska at 111.1mph (178.8km/h) – beating existing US and world records so comprehensively that the suspicious authorities refused to ratify the achievement. But the Cyclones were as unreliable as they were fast, and frequently broke down in important races. Roadster sales were hit, the firm lacked finance for further development, and Cyclone folded in 1916 after just four eventful years of production.

Cyclone (1916)	
Engine	Air-cooled sohc four-valve 45-degree V-twin
Capacity	996cc
Maximum power	25bhp @ 5000rpm
Transmission	Chain final drive
Frame	Steel single downtube
Suspension	Leaf spring front & rear
Brakes	None front, drum rear
Weight	280lb (127kg)
Top speed	85mph (137km/h)

Douglas 2.75hp

Douglas was more than a motorcycle manufacturer and built cars, tractors and aeroplane engines as well as the flat-twin motorcycles for which the Bristol marque was best known. The bikes, first produced in 1907, generally had their engines arranged with cylinders running in line with the machine, in the format of the company's first 350cc model.

A typical early Douglas was the 2.75hp Light Motor Cycle produced from about 1915, which with its narrow tyres and weight of just 169lb (77kg) was almost more like a motorised bicycle than a motorbike. That lack of weight was one reason for the 350cc twin's popularity with British World War I despatch riders, who appreciated its ability on rough ground. As one observer wrote, 'You could literally put it under your arm and carry it out of a shell hole'.

The side-valve boxer engine was rarely fitted with a clutch. The bike had to be paddled into motion before the rider put it into gear at walking pace using the tank-mounted hand lever, then accelerated using the thumb-operated throttle. Top speed in the higher of two gears was about 40mph (64km/h), and the bike's light weight helped give good handling.

Douglas often struggled financially, but by 1930 had managed to win the team prize in the International Six Days Trial, and score several successes at the Isle of Man TT. The highlight came in 1923, when Douglas won not only the Senior but also the sidecar race, with an innovative banked outfit ridden by Freddie Dixon.

Above: Douglas's flat-twin engine had cylinders in line with the bike, and featured a large flywheel on the left side.

Below: The twin's lightweight construction helped make it very manoeuvrable and was a major reason for the bike's popularity during World War I.

Indian Powerplus

L egendary long-distance ace Erwin 'Cannonball' Baker gave Indian's
  Powerplus the perfect introduction following the bike's unveiling in 1915.
  Baker rode for 3 days, 9 hours and 15 minutes to break the record for the
1655.5-mile (2663.7km) Three Flags route from Canada to Mexico, gaining much
publicity for the Springfield firm's new 998cc V-twin.

The Powerplus proved a big success when it was launched to the public in the
following year. Designer Charles Gustafson Snr's creation retained the 42-degree
cylinder that Indian had established for its V-twins, and replaced the previous
F-head (or inlet-over-exhaust) valve layout for a superior side-valve design that
increased output to a claimed 18bhp.

That extra power gave the Powerplus a top speed of over 60mph (97km/h).
The new motor was also cleaner and quieter, due to its enclosed valve gear. It had
a three-speed gearbox with a hand change and foot clutch. There was also a back-
up hand clutch, on the right handlebar because Indian's throttle was on the left.
Leaf-spring front suspension was fitted as standard, with a leaf-spring available as
an option at the rear too.

The Indian's resultant comfort was appreciated by riders including Cannonball
Baker, who also rode the Powerplus to set 24-hour records both overland in
Australia and on the board track at Cincinnati, where he covered over 1500 miles
(2413km) in a day. The dependable Powerplus remained in Indian's range until
1924, although for the last two years it was called the Standard to prevent it
overshadowing Indian's newer Chief V-twin.

*Above: The Powerplus was a fast and refined
machine by 1918 standards, featuring lights, leaf-
spring suspension front and rear, plus enclosed
valve gear for its 42-degree V-twin engine.*

Indian Powerplus (1918)	
Engine Air-cooled four-valve side-valve 42-degree V-twin	
Capacity 988cc (79.4 x 100.8mm)	
Maximum power 18bhp	
Transmission Three-speed, chain final drive	
Frame Steel single downtube	
Suspension Leaf-spring front & (optional) rear	
Brakes None front; drum rear	
Weight 410lb (186kg)	
Top speed 65mph (105km/h)	

Excelsior Super X

Excelsior's V-twins were among the world's best bikes in the last century's second decade. The Chicago firm's sophisticated roadsters were built in motorcycling's largest factory, and evaluated on its rooftop test track. Excelsior's rapid racebikes regularly beat their rivals from the Harley-Davidson and Indian firms that were fellow members of American motorcycling's unofficial 'Big Three' manufacturers.

Like Harley, Excelsior favoured a 45-degree cylinder angle for its V-twin roadsters, which began in 1908 with an 820cc model. A 992cc bike followed three years later, and by 1918 the engine with its F-head (or inlet-over-exhaust) valve layout produced about 20bhp. By this time Excelsior had introduced a three-speed gearbox and foot clutch, alongside features including leaf-spring front suspension, footboards and a sprung saddle.

The Excelsior ran well, with a top speed of about 80mph (130km/h). The firm had agreed with other American manufacturers to halt racing during World War I, but the high-speed exploits of Excelsior rider Wells Bennett provided some welcome publicity. In 1918 Bennett covered the 300-mile (483km) desert route from Los Angeles to Needles in California at an average of 42.3mph (68km/h).

Excelsior began a trend in 1925 by launching the 750cc (45 cubic inch) Super X, which triggered the growth of 750cc Class C racing. But although Excelsior restyled the Super X to good effect in 1929, the V-twin could not turn round the firm's financial problems, which worsened in the Depression shortly afterwards. In 1931, owner Ignaz Schwinn dramatically abandoned motorcycle production. The famous Excelsior marque was no more.

Above: The Super X's 750cc or 45 cubic inch engine capacity set a trend, and inspired the competitive Class C racing division.

Below: The rider of this Super X racer had no brakes to worry about, but did have to remember to give the engine some oil with the tank-mounted pump.

BSA Model E

BSA's 770cc Model E was one of the bikes with which the firm boosted its reputation in the 1920s. The big V-twin was well suited to being fitted with the sidecar that provided transport for many British families. The Model E was even offered for sale complete with a sidecar that was painted to match in the Birmingham marque's colours of green and cream.

The Model E was notable more for strength and dependability than performance. Its side-valve engine had cylinders arranged at 50 degrees, and featured a three-speed gearbox. Primary and final drive chains were enclosed in an aluminium case. The 6bhp maximum output gave a top speed of 55mph (88km/h) in solo form. Chassis specification included girder forks, rigid rear end, and a respectably light total weight figure of 350lb (159kg).

Twins including the Model E helped broaden the appeal of the Birmingham Small Arms Company. The firm had built bicycles as well as armaments for two decades before beginning motorcycle production in the early 1900s. Its first machines used bought-in engines from manufacturers including Belgium's Minerva, but by 1910 BSA had a 499cc bike powered by a 3.5hp engine of the firm's own construction.

The success of machines including the Model E prompted BSA to turn to mass-production by the mid-1920s. Alongside it BSA built bikes including the Model B or 'Round Tank', a simple side-valve 250cc single introduced in 1924, and the famous 493cc 'Sloper', named after its angled-forward cylinder, which followed two years later.

Above: Its headlight, large mudguards, footboards and efficient silencer confirmed that the BSA was built for comfort rather than performance.

Above: BSA's side-valve engine had cylinders angled at 50 degrees, and produced a maximum of 6bhp with a minimum of fuss.

BMW R32

The Bayerische Motoren Werke, which had built BMW aircraft engines during World War I, was one of many German firms that turned to motorcycle manufacture in the early 1920s, when forced to abandon aircraft work under the Treaty of Versailles. The company had employed more than 3500 people during the War, having been formed in 1917 following an alliance of two leading aircraft engine manufacturers, Otto and Rapp.

The first BMW bike was a simple motorised bicycle called the Flink. It was powered by a proprietary Kurier 148cc two-stroke engine, and was not a success. In 1921, BMW engineer Martin Stolle designed a 494cc flat-twin side-valve engine, designated the M2B15, which the Munich firm sold to other manufacturers including Victoria, Heller and Bison. The M2B15 produced 6bhp and was designed to be mounted with its cylinders running in line with the bike.

A year later the R32 was created by Max Friz, an aeroplane engineer who was one of BMW's original directors. Friz designed a new flat-twin engine that retained the 494cc capacity, but sat at 90 degrees to the previous unit, with cylinders across the frame, giving improved cooling. The engine incorporated a three-speed

Above: BMW established the transverse flat-twin layout with the firm's very first bike.

Above: The R32's drive shaft design prevented rear wheel suspension, but the twin's front end benefited from a leaf-spring system.

BMW R32 (1923)

Engine Air-cooled ohv pushrod four-valve flat-twin

Capacity 494cc (68 x 68mm)

Maximum power 8.5hp @ 3200rpm

Transmission Three-speed, shaft final drive

Frame Steel twin tube

Suspension Leaf spring front; rigid rear

Brakes Drum front; rim rear

Weight 269lb (122kg)

Top speed 55mph (88km/h)

Opposite: Large mudguards and the upturned alloy footboards helped make the first BMW an impressively clean and practical machine.

gearbox, worked by a lever to the right of the fuel tank, and shaft final drive. A steel mushroom was fitted to the top of each cylinder head to give protection in the event of a crash.

The chassis was based on a triangulated, twin-downtube steel frame. Front suspension was by a similar system to that used by Indian; a variation of the leaf-spring design that incorporated trailing links plus slim rods running up to forward-projecting laminated springs. The shaft drive meant that no rear suspension could be used so a sprung saddle was employed to provide a comfortable ride. Braking was provided by a drum on the front wheel, plus a friction device working on a dummy wheel rim at the rear.

The R32 motor produced 8.5bhp, good for a top speed of about 55mph (88km/h), and the bike was neatly finished and well built, with electric lighting and enclosed valve gear. The BMW generated great excitement when unveiled at the Paris Motorcycle Salon in 1923. Most machines of the day were assembled using parts from various sources but the R32 stood out for having clearly been designed as a complete entity. Its alloy footboards were neatly integrated with the engine and frame. The footboards' raised fronts combined with the large mudguards and the shaft final drive system to make the BMW a notably clean and practical machine.

Although expensive, the R32 was a success. More than 3000 units were sold during the next four years, establishing BMW as a serious motorcycle manufacturer. The model was developed by engineer Rudolf Schleicher to create the R37, which had an overhead-valve instead of side-valve layout, and produced a considerably increased maximum of 16bhp. Schleicher and others rode the R37 in variety of competitive events. Production of the R32 ended in 1926, but its real legacy is that well into the next century, BMW was still building bikes powered by air-cooled boxer engines.

Ner-A-Car

For a bike that in some ways was an early ancestor of modern scooters, the Ner-A-Car was a very strange device. Even the name was eccentric, though doubly appropriate. The Ner-A-Car was invented by an American named Carl Neracher. And Neracher's creation was arguably as 'Near A Car' in its concept and its level of weather protection as any two-wheeled vehicle had been when he built his first machine in 1921.

The Ner-A-Car featured motorcycling's first production example of hub-centre steering. Its twin-sided front suspension arms were connected to a low, flat chassis formed mainly from pressed steel. The rider sat upright on a sprung saddle, with feet well forward, grasping long handlebars. The engine was situated very low in the frame, which did much to give the Ner-A-Car the stability for which it became well known.

When production began at Syracuse, New York, in 1921, the engine was a 211cc air-cooled two-stroke, later enlarged to 255cc. Neracher also licensed British firm Sheffield-Simplex, producers of high quality cars, to manufacture the bike. The Surrey firm enlarged the two-stroke engine to 285cc, and also built Model B and C versions with more powerful 350cc Blackburne four-stroke engines.

In 1926, Sheffield-Simplex introduced an upmarket De-Luxe model with rear suspension, and air-cushion bucket seat, adjustable windscreen and an instrument panel. But the luxurious machine was too civilised and unusual to sell in great numbers. By the end of the 1920s production had ended in both Britain and America.

Ner-A-Car (1925)	
Engine	Air-cooled two-stroke single
Capacity	255cc (70 x 66mm)
Maximum power	4.5bhp
Transmission	Variable friction primary, chain final drive
Frame	Pressed steel
Suspension	Hub-centre front, none rear
Brakes	None front; twin drums rear
Weight	200lb (91kg)
Top speed	40mph (64km/h)

Below: Ner-A-Car's diversity of production is highlighted by the contrasting engines of the 225cc two-stroke (left) and the Model B four-stroke, both of which were produced in 1925.

Norton CS1

The CS1 was perhaps the most significant of the great single-cylinder Nortons of the 1920s and '30s. The Birmingham firm's side-valve and pushrod-operated bikes had already scored many race wins at the Isle of Man TT and elsewhere. But it was the CS1, with its overhead camshaft valve operation, that reignited the marque following its launch in 1927.

At that time Norton was struggling, following the death two years earlier of founder James Lansdowne 'Pa' Norton, following long-standing heart problems. The firm's ageing pushrod single engine was becoming less competitive. It was redesigned with an overhead cam by Walter Moore, Norton's talented development engineer and race team boss.

Moore's 490cc CS1 (Cam Shaft 1) engine retained traditional long-stroke dimensions of 79 x 100mm, and replaced the pushrods with an overhead cam, driven via a shaft running in a vertical tower. It produced 20bhp and was an immediate success when introduced in 1927. Norton's Alec Bennett won that year's Senior TT, and Stanley Woods broke the lap record on a similar machine. The following year the CS1 was offered as a sporting roadster.

Norton was rocked when Moore quit to join Germany's NSU, whose later 500SS resembled the CS1 so closely that Norton workers claimed NSU stood for 'Norton Spares Used'. In 1931 Norton's Arthur Carroll redesigned the single's camshaft drive, switching the exhaust pipe from the left side to the right. Norton dominated the 1932 Senior TT, and the following year released a roadgoing version, the International, that remained successful for the rest of the decade.

Above: The CS1's highlight was its 490cc engine's overhead camshaft, driven by the bevel shaft that ran down the right side of the cylinder.

Above: The silver-tanked CS1's exhaust pipe exited to the left, which made the single easily distinguishable from the later International with its right-sided pipe.

Henderson Model KJ

The Model KJ, known as the Streamline, was the last and best of the magnificent four-cylinder machines built by Henderson over almost two decades. The KJ, designed by Arthur Constantine, was released in 1929. It retained the 1301cc (79 cubic inch) capacity of Henderson's previous Model K four, as well as the marque's traditional engine layout of cylinders in line with the bike.

That Streamline nickname came from its smooth styling, courtesy of a low seat and a rounded fuel tank that incorporated the instruments in its top. Engine modifications included new inlet-over-exhaust valve layout with enclosed rocker gear, plus improved cooling due to heavier fins. Peak power output rose from the Model K's 28 to 40bhp, giving the Streamline a genuine top speed of 100mph (161km/h) plus smooth high-speed cruising ability.

Other notable features were leading-link forks, the front brake that Henderson had introduced in the previous year, and a lighting system that included illumination for the tank-mounted speedometer. The KJ was fast, luxurious and lived up to Henderson's reputation for quality, which had been maintained ever since 1912, when brothers Tom and William Henderson had built their first four-cylinder machine in Detroit.

Since then Hendersons had set numerous long-distance records. The glamorous bikes had also attracted celebrity owners including Henry Ford, who had paid the full price of $370 after being refused a discount. But Ford had the last laugh, when his Model T's success decimated the US motorcycle industry. Owners Schwinn, who had bought the firm and merged it with Excelsior in 1917, ended production in 1931.

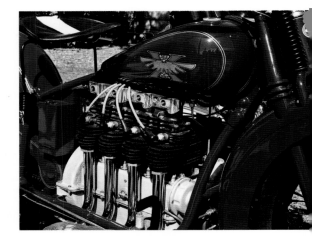

Above: The Model KJ's 1301cc four-cylinder engine featured enclosed valve gear plus heavy finning of its iron barrels, to aid cooling.

Below: The Streamline was a handsome machine, earning its nickname with a clean look that included a rounded tank and low, sprung saddle.

Indian Scout

The middleweight Scout was a long-running success for Indian, confirming designer Charles B Franklin's belief that many American riders would appreciate a smaller V-twin than the firm's 998cc Powerplus, from which it was descended. The original Scout, launched in 1919, had a 615cc (37 cubic inch) side-valve engine in Indian's familiar 42-degree layout. It produced 11bhp, was capable of 60mph (97km/h), handled better than the Powerplus and soon gained a reputation for reliability.

An important Scout development came in 1927 when its engine was enlarged to 750cc (45ci) to compete with Excelsior's Super X. The following year's 101 Scout combined a long wheelbase and low seating position to deliver outstanding handling, and became very popular. Its 22bhp engine gave a top speed of 75mph (121km/h), and its reliability justified the Indian advertising line: 'You can't wear out an Indian Scout'. Other innovations included a drum front brake, plus new carburettor and oil pump designs.

Numerous Scout variants were introduced over the years, not all with good results. The Standard Scout of 1932 was heavy; the 500cc Scout Pony lacked power. Indian had more joy in 1934 with the Sport Scout, which retained the traditional 750cc capacity and combined lively performance with agile handling. It responded well to tuning and was ridden successfully in TT events, hill climbs and Class C dirt-track races. In 1940, Indian fitted the Sport Scout with big 'skirted' mudguards. Production ended two years later but stripped-down Scouts were still winning races in the 1950s.

Above: This 1931 Scout features leaf-spring front suspension, hard-tail rear and a 750cc V-twin engine with 42-degree cylinder angle.

Indian Sport Scout (1934)	
Engine Air-cooled four-valve side-valve 42-degree V-twin	
Capacity 744cc (73 x 89mm)	
Maximum power 22bhp	
Transmission Three-speed, chain final drive	
Frame Steel twin downtube	
Suspension Girder front; none rear	
Brakes Drum front & rear	
Weight 450lb (204kg)	
Top speed 80mph (129km/h)	

Rudge Ulster

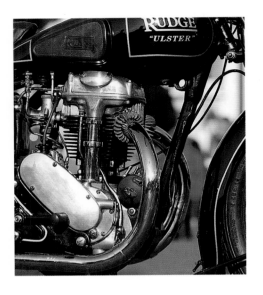

The best known of Rudge's numerous rapid and refined 500cc singles was the Ulster, named after the 1928 Ulster Grand Prix victory by Graham Walker, the Coventry firm's works rider and sales manager (and father of TV commentator Murray). Walker averaged over 80mph (129km/h) to win on a new machine whose engine used four valves arranged around a central spark plug. Rudge responded by introducing a 500cc four-valve roadster single, the Ulster, for the following year.

In 1930 Rudge made another advance with a new single-cylinder engine whose four valves were arranged radially, and which gave the firm a one-two-three in that year's Junior TT. Factory riders Walker, HG Tyrell Smith and Ernie Nott won many big races, and the firm also produced a TT Replica that was raced successfully by privateers, in 250, 350 and 500cc capacities. The Ulster adopted a semi-radial valve layout that boosted its power output to 30bhp, giving a top speed of over 95mph (145km/h), which allowed the firm to advertise it as: 'probably the fastest 500cc motorcycle in normal production'.

Straight-line performance was not the Ulster's only attribute, for it was a notably sophisticated and comfortable machine. Its engine featured an alloy cylinder head, enclosed valve gear, and four-speed gearbox. Braking was Rudge's linked system, by which the foot pedal worked the front and rear drums, and the handlebar lever operated the front drum. Despite this and other refined touches including a hand-operated centre-stand, Rudge could not sell enough bikes to survive the difficult financial climate of the 1930s.

Above: The Ulster's semi-radial four-valve head meant that its single 500cc cylinder required twin exhaust pipes.

Below: As well as being fast, the Rudge roadster was a sophisticated machine with enclosed valve gear, four-speed gearbox and linked brake system.

Crocker

Above: Two-tone paintwork and a notably lean look gave Crocker's powerful V-twin plenty of style to go with its impressive performance.

The light, powerful and cleverly designed V-twins built by Albert Crocker's company were some of the best bikes produced before World War II. Crocker was a fine rider, engineer and designer who worked for Thor before becoming an Indian dealer, latterly in Los Angeles. After hiring another talented engineer named Paul Bigsby in 1928, he began building bikes for speedway racing, powered firstly by Indian's 750cc Scout engine, then by 500cc singles of the duo's own design.

In 1936 Crocker began production of a sports roadster whose 998cc V-twin engine's layout owed much to that of the single, with cylinders at 45 degrees and overhead valves with exposed springs. The three-speed gearbox was cast as an integral part of the frame. Peak output was an impressive 50bhp. Crocker's racing background showed in the V-twin's relatively light weight of 480lb (218kg), achieved by using aluminium for parts including the fuel tank, engine cases and footboards.

The Crocker was stylish and fast, with a top speed of about 110mph (176km/h) and acceleration to match. It was 10bhp more powerful than Harley-Davidson's new Model 61E, launched the same year. The hand-built machines also handled well, with the aid of girder front suspension. Al Crocker's problem was that at over $500 they were also very expensive, costing $150 more than the mass-produced Harley. He hoped that Indian, with which he still had links, would buy the rights to build the V-twin. But World War II arrived instead and Crocker abandoned V-twin production having built fewer than 100 bikes.

Crocker V-twin (1936)	
Engine Air-cooled ohv four-valve pushrod 45-degree V-twin	
Capacity 998cc	
Maximum power 50bhp @ 5800rpm	
Transmission Three-speed, chain final drive	
Frame Steel single downtube	
Suspension Springer forks; rigid rear	
Brakes Drum front & rear	
Weight 480lb (218kg)	
Top speed 110mph (176km/h)	

Excelsior Manxman

Much of British marque Excelsior's production comprised small-capacity two-strokes, but the Coventry firm had a big hit in the 1930s with the Manxman, an overhead-cam four-stroke single. Although the Manxman did not win a TT, it was a fast and successful racebike, and also a popular roadster.

Ironically the Manxman was not Excelsior's most glamorous bike of the time. The firm's innovative 250cc radial-valve 'Mechanical Marvel' had taken a spectacular victory at the 1933 Junior TT, ridden by Sid Gleave. But the Marvel was too complex for production, so Excelsior boss Eric Walker and engine designer Ike Hatch collaborated to create the Manxman, whose simpler 246cc single-cylinder engine used two valves, with shaft-and-bevel drive to an overhead camshaft.

The Manxman was introduced in 1935 in 250 and 350cc capacities, with a 500cc model following a year later. The 350cc model produced 23bhp and was good for 85mph (137km/h). Bikes could be purchased either in competition specification, for grass-track or road racing, or in street-legal form. The roadster had a more upright riding position plus a Miller Dynamag lighting system.

Excelsior guaranteed that production Manxman competition bikes were 'genuine racing machines, not replicas'. They were advertised as 'hand built and tested by our racing and experimental department'. At the 1938 TT, the 250cc Manxman took second to seventh places in the Junior race, behind German marque DKW's supercharged works two-stroke. Manxman production ended in 1939, although Excelsior restarted its two-stroke operation after World War II and continued until the early 1960s.

Above: The Manxman's overhead cam was driven by shaft and bevel drive, complete with three-legged Manx logo on the cover.

Below: This 1936 Manxman is a 250cc model, the smallest of the three-bike range, and lacks the lights that would normally have been fitted for roadgoing use.

Harley-Davidson Model 61E

The Model 61E that Harley-Davidson launched in 1936 was arguably the most significant bike the Milwaukee firm has ever produced. As Harley's first purpose-built overhead-valve V-twin, the 61E was the machine from which all subsequent models evolved. And the new machine, with its superior performance and specification, gave Harley an advantage over Indian and helped the company recover from the difficult times of the Depression.

Nicknamed the Knucklehead after the distinctive shape of its alloy rocker boxes, the Model 61E was built around a new 989cc (61 cubic inches, hence the designation) engine that retained the marque's 45-degree cylinder angle. Its new recirculating lubrication system, in place of the previous total-loss arrangement, was a big advance.

So was the overhead valve set-up that helped give a peak output of 37bhp, or 40bhp for the 61EL model with its higher compression ratio. That gave the EL a genuine 100mph (161km/h) top speed – recorded on Harley's first standard-fitment speedometer, incorporated into the top of the fuel tank with its classical art deco logo.

Other key features included a four-speed gearbox, new twin-cradle frame, and improved springer front suspension system. The 61E's introduction did not run completely smoothly, as the bike suffered from teething problems including oil leaks and issues regarding frame strength. But the model quickly became popular, its 1936 sales total of almost 2000 exceeding Harley's expectations. In 1941, the first of many major revamps resulted in the 1213cc Model 74F. Many other changes followed, but the influence of that first Knucklehead is still felt today.

Above: *The Model 61E's key feature was its sophisticated 989cc Knucklehead engine, complete with overhead valves and recirculating oil system.*

Harley-Davidson Model 61EL (1936)	
Engine Air-cooled ohv four-valve pushrod 45-degree V-twin	
Capacity 988cc (84 x 88.9mm)	
Maximum power 40bhp @ 4800rpm	
Transmission Four-speed, chain final drive	
Frame Steel twin downtube	
Suspension Springer forks; rigid rear	
Brakes Drum front & rear	
Weight 515lb (234kg)	
Top speed 100mph (161km/h)	

Brough Superior

T he mighty V-twins from George Brough's Nottingham workshop were the most glamorous and exotic motorcycles of the 1920s and '30s. In their maker's own words, the Brough Superior was a 'big solo machine, made up to an ideal and not down to a price'. The bikes certainly had the performance to match their high price.

Brough combined his own frames with V-twin powerplants from JAP and Matchless to create innovative, fast and expensive roadburners. Bought-in components were not only the best available, but in many cases had to be improved still further before being accepted for Brough use.

George Brough was a fine rider as well as engineer, and won many races, sprints and hill climbs, as did other notable 'Brufsup' riders including Eric Fernihough, Freddie Dixon and Bert Le Vack. He also excelled in marketing and was not notably modest, highlighted when he named his machine the Superior – to the annoyance of his father, a manufacturer of flat-twin bikes himself, who retorted: 'I suppose that makes mine the Brough Inferior?'

The 1924 Brough Superior catalogue stated that: 'It is very satisfying to know that you are astride a machine which, if you wish, can leave behind anything on wheels.' That was a bold claim, as were others such as 'It is actually possible to ride hands off at 60mph', and 'It starts first kick from stone cold'. But if anyone could justify such statements it was Brough, who used the line 'the Rolls-Royce of Motorcycles' in his advertising, and was allowed to continue after a displeased

Above: Broughs' exotic nature and high-quality construction justified the firm's advertising boast: 'the Rolls-Royce of motorcycles'.

Below: A big chromed fuel tank was almost as much of a distinctive Brough Superior feature as the V-twin engine.

Above: Brough's use of premium quality cycle parts gave the Superior excellent handling and 'hands-off' stability at speed.

Rolls executive had arrived at the Nottingham workshop to find show bikes being assembled by workers wearing white gloves.

Approximately 3000 Superiors were produced during Brough's two decades in business. Many of those were the SS80, named after its 80mph (128km/h) top speed. It used a side-valve V-twin engine, latterly a 990cc, 50-degree Matchless powerplant that incorporated numerous modifications from the units fitted to the Matchless Model X. As well as obvious features such as the Brough Superior name on the tappet and timing covers, the SS80 had modified cylinder porting and a different exhaust system.

Brough's more powerful, overhead-valve SS100 was initially powered by a 980cc, 45bhp JAP engine, and was delivered with a signed guarantee that the bike had been timed at over 100mph (161km/h) for a quarter of a mile. Fewer than 400 were built. Even more special versions included the SS100 Alpine Grand Sports, built for fast touring, and the racing Pendine, with high-compression engine and guaranteed 110mph (176km/h) top speed.

Brough continually updated the Superior's specification, introducing optional rear suspension in 1928, foot gear change in 1935 and a four-speed Norton gearbox a year later. His many innovations included flyscreens, twin headlamps, crashbars and panniers. T E Shaw, alias 'Lawrence of Arabia', was a devoted Brough enthusiast – and sadly one of the least fortunate. Lawrence, who owned a special stainless-steel petrol tank which he fitted to his series of Superiors, died in 1935 after crashing his SS100.

Brough Superior SS80 (1937)	
Engine Air-cooled side-valve four-valve 50-degree V-twin	
Capacity 990cc (84 x 90mm)	
Maximum power 35bhp @ 4000rpm	
Transmission Four-speed, chain final drive	
Frame Steel single downtube	
Suspension Girder forks; plunger rear	
Brakes Drum front & rear	
Weight 420lb (191kg)	
Top speed 80mph (129km/h)	

Norton Big Four

Above: *By the time this bike was built in 1937, the Big Four's specification included lights and a saddle-style fuel tank.*

The Big Four was one of the best known and longest lasting of all Norton's early singles, but by no means one of the most glamorous. The 633cc Big Four earned its name because the original, 1907-model machine, powered by James Lansdowne Norton's first ever engine, produced just four horsepower.

The slow-revving single's reputation for efficiency and reliability was forged by the original model. Early Big Fours had a bicycle-style frame and belt final drive. By 1927 final drive was by chain, enclosed in a pressed-steel case containing oil, and the stirrup front brake had been replaced by a drum. But although the Big Four remained a favourite of 'Pa' Norton, it badly needed updating.

Changes over the next few years included a shorter wheelbase frame and a modern saddle-style fuel tank. By 1937 the engine benefited from a four-speed gearbox and enclosed valve gear, but its output had not increased significantly. The Big Four was good for 60mph (97km/h) but felt slightly slower than in earlier years, due to its extra weight plus the demands of its gearbox and the dynamo that had been introduced to power its lighting.

Later Big Fours were fitted with Norton's famed Roadholder forks, which improved handling. Other changes including a dual-seat kept the model going for a few more years, but the end finally came for all Norton's side-valvers in 1954. By remaining in production for almost half a century, the softly-tuned touring single had played an important part in the Norton story.

Above: *Norton's traditional silver-and-black paint scheme, made famous by factory racebikes, helped give the slow-revving single a deceptively sporty look.*

Indian Four

Few bikes could match the performance or comfort of Indian's Four, which was created in 1927 when the Springfield giant took over the failed Ace firm. The four-cylinder Ace had been designed by William Henderson, co-founder of Henderson, and had earned a fine reputation before his death in a testing crash in 1922. Its 1265cc engine produced 35bhp, ran smoothly and gave a top speed of 80mph (129km/h).

Indian rebadged the four as the Indian Ace, and offered it in the firm's traditional dark red as well as blue. Over the next few years the bike was renamed the Indian Four, and updated with a stronger crankshaft, new frame, and leaf-spring front suspension. For 1932 it was comprehensively revised, with more streamlined styling plus a stronger frame. But as well as gaining some power the Four had put on weight.

By this time Indian was struggling through the Depression, and built a record low total of 1667 bikes the following year, of which fewer than ten per cent were the pricey Four. When the US economy picked up, Indian blundered by reinventing the model as the Model 436 Four, with a reversed 'exhaust-over-inlet' valve arrangement. It looked messy, proved unpopular and was rapidly replaced.

The final Fours, built in the early 1940s, combined conventional valve gear with Indian's trademark giant skirted mudguards. They were comfortable and stylish, but slow and heavy. When Indian restarted civilian bike production after the War, the Four was no longer part of the range.

Above: *This Indian Four motor was produced in 1940 and has been updated with a foot-operated gear change in place of its original hand change.*

Below: *The handsome early Four owed its engine layout and much of its look to the Ace, but the leaf-spring front suspension was an Indian addition.*

Triumph Speed Twin

T he Speed Twin changed the face of motorcycling in a way that only a handful of bikes have done. Triumph chief engineer Edward Turner's 498cc parallel twin was launched into a world of mostly single-cylinder machines in 1937. Its immediate popularity gave Triumph a huge and lasting boost, and resulted in rival British manufacturers basing their ranges on the parallel-twin engine for the next three decades.

One short blast on the Speed Twin was usually all a rider needed to appreciate the benefits of a quick, torquey machine that was notably smoother than comparable singles. It was also lighter than Triumph's own Tiger 90 single, and barely more expensive. And Turner's legendary eye for style ensured that the maroon-and-chrome machine looked the part too. Given all that, it's no surprise that the Speed Twin and its descendants dominated the post-War motorcycling scene.

The key to the Speed Twin's success was that sweet-running vertical twin engine. Twin camshafts, driven by gear from the crankshaft, operated pushrods with tubes set into the vees between the cylinders at the front and rear. The

Triumph Speed Twin (1938)	
Engine	Air-cooled ohv four-valve pushrod parallel twin
Capacity	498cc (63 x 80mm)
Maximum power	29bhp @ 6000rpm
Transmission	Four-speed, chain final drive
Frame	Steel twin downtube
Suspension	Girder front; rigid rear
Brakes	Drum front & rear
Weight	365lb (166kg)
Top speed	95mph (153km/h)

Above: The Speed Twin's powerful, compact and reasonably smooth-running 498cc engine triggered the parallel-twin revolution that transformed motorcycling in the 1940s.

Right: This 1946-model Speed Twin features the telescopic forks that replaced the original girders when Triumph restarted production after the War. Other changes included a larger fuel tank, magneto ignition and restyled headlight.

Below: With its lean and attractive lines, enhanced by a touch of chrome, the Speed Twin demonstrated Triumph design chief Edward Turner's famed eye for style.

engine was not in a particularly high state of tune, which helped make it pleasantly smooth-running, but still produced a very respectable peak output of 29bhp at 6000rpm.

From the moment the Speed Twin was launched, its engine was much praised for its flexibility, which allowed the bike to pull from below 30mph (48km/h) in top gear, and even trickle along at slower speed in top without complaint. The Triumph was fast, too. The 1937 model was tested by *The Motor Cycle* at 107mph (172km/h) – 'truly an amazing figure for a fully equipped 500' – although 95mph (153km/h) was a more typical figure.

Another important feature of the motor was its compact size, which allowed it to be fitted into the Tiger 90's single-downtube frame, without altering the line of the drive chain. As well as reducing Triumph's development costs, that helped ensure the twin's acceptance in the conservative two-wheeled world of the late 1930s and '40s. The chassis gave good handling, although the unsprung rear end had a tendency to bounce over bumps at speed. The front and rear drum brakes were very efficient.

The Speed Twin was an immediate hit, and in 1939 was joined in the range by the tuned Tiger 100, named in typically shrewd Turner fashion after its 100mph (161km/h) top speed. The War soon put paid to Triumph's production of civilian machines, but both models were revived in 1946. For its comeback the Speed Twin was fitted with telescopic forks instead of the original girders; a larger, four-gallon petrol tank; and magneto ignition (instead of the original magdyno) with a dynamo to power the restyled headlight.

Both the Speed Twin and Tiger 100 would remain hugely successful throughout the 1940s, being joined in 1950 by the Thunderbird, with its torquier 650cc engine. By this time most other British manufacturers had joined in by developing parallel twins of their own. The Speed Twin and its descendants had shown the way forward.

Chapter 2

Post-War Classics

Ariel Square Four

Ariel's Square Four retained its name and distinctive engine layout through its long production life, during which it was repeatedly updated from the original 497cc model of 1931 to the 997cc 4G MkII of 1958. Throughout that 27-year period, which saw a doubling of engine capacity and a huge increase in performance, the Square Four maintained its assets of four-cylinder power and smoothness with compact size. Unfortunately for Ariel, the model's disadvantages – high production costs and the problems of cooling the sheltered rear cylinders – also remained.

The Square Four was the brainchild of young design genius Edward Turner, who showed several factories sketches of his new engine – essentially two pairs of parallel twins, with crankshafts geared together – before Ariel boss Jack Sangster gave him the go-ahead. The resultant powerplant ran very smoothly, and was so compact that it fitted into a frame almost identical to that of Ariel's 500cc single.

That first Square Four was enthusiastically received when unveiled at London's Olympia Show in 1930. It featured a chain-driven overhead camshaft and exhaust manifolds integral with the cylinder head, so only two pipes emerged from the engine. Turner's original design had used an integral three-speed gearbox, but the production bike used a four-speed box, with hand change.

Above: The Square Four 4G's 997cc engine produced 34bhp and was heavily finned in an attempt to cool the rear cylinders.

Below: This 1952-model 'Squariel' was a stylish bike whose flexible engine's performance justified the firm's boast of 'Ten to a hundred in top gear'.

Above: The later Square Four 4G MkII announced its four-cylinder engine layout with a quartet of exhaust downpipes. This 1959-model bike was one of the last to be built before Ariel abandoned four-stroke production.

For 1932 the engine was enlarged to 597cc, the smaller engine being dropped shortly afterwards. In this form the Square Four produced 24bhp at 6000rpm, and stayed smooth to its top speed of 85mph (136km/h). Despite its high price the 'Squariel' was popular, especially with sidecar enthusiasts. But its flywheels were too light, and cylinder head cooling was a problem.

Turner left for Triumph, and for 1937 Ariel's new chief engineer Val Page designed revised 597cc and 997cc models, the 4F and 4G. They featured longer-stroke dimensions, pushrod valve operation, and extra cylinder head finning plus a tunnel between the cylinders, to allow cooling air to the rear cylinders. A Solex carburettor, placed conventionally behind the motor, replaced the previous forward-mounted Amal. The larger 4G produced 34bhp and was very flexible, prompting Ariel's famous advertising line: 'Ten to a hundred in top gear'. But reliability problems lingered.

Ariel reduced weight and improved cooling after World War II with a new all-aluminium engine, and in 1953 introduced the comprehensively revised Square Four 4G MkII. This was a stylish bike that emphasised its engine layout with four separate exhaust downpipes for the first time. Even in this final form the engine was prone to overheat in traffic, but the impressively broad power delivery allowed the rider to enjoy the bike's smooth cruising ability with little need to use the four-speed gearbox.

By now the Ariel had adopted telescopic forks and plunger rear suspension, but the Square Four's handling did not match the performance of its engine. Even so, the 4G MkII was a notably smooth and luxurious machine. Production finally ended in 1958, when Ariel abandoned four-strokes to build the Leader two-stroke. The Square Four's reputation as a high-class tourer lives on.

Ariel Square Four 4G Mk1 (1952)	
Engine Air-cooled ohv eight-valve pushrod square-four	
Capacity 997cc (65 x 75mm)	
Maximum power 34bhp @ 5400rpm	
Transmission Four-speed, chain final drive	
Frame Steel twin downtube	
Suspension Telescopic front; plunger rear	
Brakes Drum front & rear	
Weight 433lb (197kg)	
Top speed 100mph (160km/h)	

Scott Flying Squirrel

'Silence, performance, simplicity and smoothness give the Scott an individuality which cannot be rivalled by any other make of machine.' the Flying Squirrel's brochure enthused in the 1940s, with little fear of contradiction. The Yorkshire firm's 596cc, liquid-cooled two-stroke parallel twin was unlike any other bike, continuing a tradition of innovative engineering that stretched back to the machines with which founder Alfred Angas Scott had started production back in 1904.

The Flying Squirrel was launched in 1926, three years after Scott's death. It featured a conventional petrol tank and frame, in place of previous models' cylindrical tanks and open frames. The firm's trademark engine format was retained, in 498 and 596cc capacities. The larger model produced 25bhp, giving a 70mph (112km/h) top speed with impressive smoothness and a unique high-pitched 'yowl' from the exhaust.

After World War II Scott briefly resumed production of the rigid framed Flying Squirrel, updated from girder to telescopic forks. But the bikes were heavy and underpowered, the 596cc engine having barely been updated since gaining detachable cylinder heads in 1934. The Squirrel was also expensive and not particularly reliable, and few were sold.

In 1950, struggling Scott was bought by Birmingham-based enthusiast Matt Holder. He added a swing-arm frame and continued developing and selling Squirrels in tiny numbers right up until 1978. The Squirrel's remarkable production life of more than half a century highlighted the advanced design and unique appeal of the original machine.

Above: *The softly-tuned Flying Squirrel had a much more solid, touring feel than the Yorkshire firm's sportier early models, and needed its engine flexibility because the gearbox had only three speeds.*

Below: *The Flying Squirrel retained Scott's traditional two-stroke parallel twin engine layout, but had a conventional fuel tank and frame instead of the old bike's cylindrical tank and open frame.*

Sunbeam S7 De Luxe

Sunbeam billed the S7 as 'the world's most magnificent motor cycle' on its launch in 1947, and the mist-green tandem twin was certainly an impressive looking machine. Designer Erling Poppe's 487cc engine featured overhead-camshaft valve operation and shaft final drive. The chassis promised luxury with its balloon tyres and skirted mudguards. The S7 was a glamorous flagship for the upmarket Sunbeam marque, recently acquired by the giant BSA group.

But the S7, whose emphasis on comfort had been inspired by BMW R75 flat twins captured during the War, was a disaster. For a 500cc machine its general performance and 75mph (120km/h) top speed were unimpressive. The S7 was heavy at almost 440lb (200kg), handled poorly due partly to its fat tyres, and had poor brakes. Its 25bhp motor used a lot of fuel and was unreliable. Its problems included overheating, cracked cylinder liners and main bearing failure – all especially unwelcome on a bike costing over £200.

Sunbeam's response came in 1949, when the firm not only introduced the cheaper and more conventional S8, but also the S7 De Luxe. This had a redesigned engine with a deeper oil sump, new cylinder liners and larger rubber mounts. The chassis was also improved, most importantly gaining conventional front forks with internal springs and hydraulic damping. Some of the old problems remained, and the S7 De Luxe never sold in large numbers. But it was more reliable and handled better than its predecessor, and had much to offer as a stylish, comfortable roadster.

Above: The S7's big mudguards, fat tyres, tandem-twin engine and mist-green paintwork gave a unique look. This 1949-model De Luxe features the conventional hydraulic forks that replaced the original model's inefficient undamped units.

Sunbeam S7 De Luxe (1949)

Engine	Air-cooled sohc four-valve tandem twin
Capacity	487cc (70 x 63.5mm)
Maximum power	25bhp @ 5800rpm
Transmission	Four-speed, shaft final drive
Frame	Steel twin downtube
Suspension	Telescopic front; plunger rear
Brakes	Drum front & rear
Weight	440lb (200kg)
Top speed	75mph (120km/h)

Vincent Rapide

Vincent's thundering V-twins were the world's fastest and finest roadsters in the 1940s and early '50s, combining exhilarating high performance with stable handling, excellent braking and long-distance cruising ability. The machines created at Vincent's base at Stevenage in Hertfordshire were also stylish, well built and inevitably expensive.

Philip Vincent had started his motorcycle operation in 1928 after buying the defunct HRD marque. Engines from JAP, Villiers and Rudge were fitted until 1934 when Vincent and his Australian chief engineer Phil Irving produced the firm's own unit, a 500cc 'high cam' single, which was used to power the sporty Comet and touring Meteor.

Irving designed Vincent's first V-twin in 1936 by combining two Comet cylinders at 47 degrees. The resultant 998cc Rapide produced 45bhp and was capable of an impressive 110mph (177km/h), although its power led to

Below: This Series C Rapide, produced in 1950, featured Vincent's Girdraulic front forks instead of the previous Series B model's Brampton girders.

transmission problems. It was nicknamed the 'Snarling Beast', and also the 'Plumber's Nightmare' due to its mass of external oil lines.

Following World War II, Vincent introduced the Series B Rapide, powered by a new engine with cylinders at 50 degrees, and unit-construction engine and gearbox. The engine formed a stressed member of the chassis, so no frame downtubes were required. The Rapide was a superb machine, its blend of power plus fine handling from its more compact chassis giving performance that no other roadster could match.

The tester from *Motor Cycle* wrote of the Rapide in 1947 that: 'there has never been a production model with so much to commend it as a road-burner's dream. From 40mph up to the maximum of over 100mph there is thrilling performance available at the twist of the grip... Though the big engine and high gearing suggest easy, loping, fussless mile-eating, there is searing acceleration available if required. Standing start getaways against the watch provide a memorable thrill and leave a black line of rubber on the road surface.'

The Series C Rapide followed in 1948, featuring Vincent's Girdraulic forks in place of the previous Brampton girders. A hydraulic damping unit was added between the diagonally mounted, side-by-side rear shock units, to assist the original friction dampers. The Rapide's thick dual-seat and efficient suspension made the bike comfortable on the long, high-speed trips that were its speciality.

Even faster was the tuned Black Shadow, whose 55bhp black-finished engine gave a top speed of over 120mph (192km/h), recorded on a large Smith's speedometer calibrated to 150mph (241km/h). American ace Rollie Free famously reached that speed on Vincent's race-specification Black Lightning, after stripping to swimming trunks and shoes to set a world record for unsupercharged bikes at just over 150.313mph (241.85km/h). Other legendary Vincents include Gunga Din, Nero and the supercharged Super Nero ridden by George Brown.

Vincent's enduring problem was that the bikes were unprofitable, despite their high prices. In 1955 the firm introduced Series D models, the Black Knight and tuned Black Prince, but the public was not yet ready for their futuristic, all-enveloping bodywork. Sales were slow, and Vincent abandoned production before the end of that year.

Above: *The Rapide was a magnificently fast and long-legged roadburner that was happy cruising at high speed for long distances, and had the stability to match.*

Vincent Rapide Series C (1949)	
Engine Air-cooled ohv four-valve 50-degree V-twin	
Capacity 998cc (84 x 90mm)	
Maximum power 45bhp @ 5300rpm	
Transmission Four-speed, chain final drive	
Frame Steel spine	
Suspension Girder front; twin shocks rear	
Brakes Twin drums front & rear	
Weight 455lb (207kg)	
Top speed 110mph (177km/h)	

Left: *With its black paintwork, purposeful look and big V-twin engine the Rapide was a stylish and tidy looking machine that had long ago lost its 'Plumber's Nightmare' nickname.*

Harley-Davidson WL45

Alongside its large-capacity V-twins, Harley-Davidson also built smaller 'Forty-fives' – the 45 cubic inch (750cc) machines that played an important part in the firm's history. The first Forty-fives, the D series, were introduced in 1928 to compete with machines of that capacity from Excelsior and Indian. In 1937 the side-valve V-twin was restyled and updated to create the W series. Performance was unexceptional but the W45 was well built and strong. Its success helped sustain Harley through the Depression of the 1930s.

As the WLA, the Forty-five also made an excellent military bike, of which an estimated 80,000 were employed during World War II. After the War, many ex-army bikes were converted for civilian use, which did much to popularise Harleys in many countries. The Forty-five also formed the basis for the Milwaukee firm's successful Class C racing machines.

The WL initials denoted a sportier version of the basic W45, with slightly raised compression increasing power to 25bhp. The three-speed gearbox was operated by a hand lever, with a foot clutch. In 1949 Harley introduced its Girdraulic damping system on the WL's springer front forks, in place of the simple friction damper used previously.

The WL had a sprung saddle and no rear suspension but it was quite comfortable, handled well and combined modest acceleration with a top speed of 75mph (120km/h). It remained in production until 1952, when it was replaced by the Model K, whose engine retained the 45ci capacity but featured a four-speed gearbox, foot-operated change and hand clutch.

Above: Harley's 750cc side-valve engine produced only 25bhp but was robust, as its popularity during World War II confirmed.

Below: The WL's hard-tail frame helped give even the softly tuned 'Forty-five' a fairly muscular appearance, and the sprung saddle provided a reasonably comfortable ride.

Gilera Saturno

Above: With its lean lines and Italian racing red paintwork the Saturno Sport was a very stylish machine. This bike dates from 1950, two years before Gilera updated the single with telescopic forks and twin shocks.

Gilera's greatest bikes of the 1950s were the mighty four-cylinder racers that won six 500cc world championships, but the Italian factory's outstanding roadsters were more simple singles of similar capacity. The best known of those was the Saturno, which was launched in 1946 and remained popular through the following decade due to its combination of style, agility, reliability and lively performance.

The Saturno was designed by Giuseppe Salmaggi, and was a development of the so-called 'eight-bolt' (Otto Bulloni) single that had been Gilera's main 500cc machine in the late 1930s. The 499cc engine had pushrod-operated valves closed by hairpin springs, and a four-speed gearbox. Two roadgoing versions were built. The Sport had an aluminium cylinder head, produced 22bhp and was good for 85mph (137km/h). The Touring model was in a lower state of tune and used a cast-iron cylinder head.

Early Saturnos had girder forks and Gilera's own brand of rear suspension: horizontal springs in tubes, with friction dampers. Telescopic forks and vertical shocks were introduced in the early 1950s. The bike became popular thanks to its excellent roadgoing performance and some impressive racing results, the first of which was Carlo Bandirola's win at the Sanremo circuit in 1947, which led to the Saturno racer being known as the Sanremo.

Saturnos were not competitive at Grand Prix level but were raced successfully in Italy throughout the 1950s. Production ended in 1959, after sales of the single had been hit by the introduction of the similarly priced Fiat 500 car.

Gilera Saturno Sport (1950)	
Engine	Air-cooled ohv 2-valve pushrod single
Capacity	499cc (84 x 90mm)
Maximum power	22hp @ 5000rpm
Transmission	Four-speed, chain final drive
Frame	Steel single downtube
Suspension	Girder front; horizontal springs rear
Brakes	Drum front & rear
Weight	385lb (175kg)
Top speed (road trim)	85mph (137km/h)

Moto Guzzi Airone

Moto Guzzi's little 250cc Airone was one of the most popular Italian roadsters of the 1940s and early '50s – a golden era for Guzzi, when the firm's horizontal single-cylinder racebikes won a string of 250 and 350cc world championships. That engine layout had characterised the Mandello marque ever since Carlo Guzzi and his friend Giorgio Parodi had built their the first machines, the 'GP' or Guzzi-Parodi racer of 1920 and the roadgoing Normale that had followed.

Above: The Airone's 250cc engine was one of the smaller examples of Guzzi's trademark flat single, and like the other versions incorporated an external 'bacon slicer' flywheel.

The Airone – Heron in English – was launched in 1939, based on a roadster called the 250 PE. The pushrod-operated single produced a claimed 9.5bhp, giving a top speed of 60mph (97km/h). The bike weighed just 297lb (135kg) and was well equipped, featuring telescopic forks and large mudguards, plus legshields as standard equipment.

There was one Airone model until 1949, when the Airone Sport was introduced, featuring a hotted-up engine with new camshaft, bigger carburettor and higher compression ratio. The Sport produced 13.5bhp at 6000rpm, a 4bhp increase on the standard model, which became the Turismo. The Sport cornered and stopped well thanks to a new chassis incorporating a tubular rather than pressed-steel frame, plus 19-inch Borrani wheels and larger drum brakes.

Guzzi modified the single several times, notably by uprating the Turismo with more power and the Sport's tubular-steel frame. But those changes couldn't maintain the Airone's popularity in the mid-1950s, in the face of opposition from 125 and 175cc models that offered similar or better performance at a lower price. Production eventually ended in 1957.

Below: This stylish Airone Sport was built in 1951, the year that Bruno Ruffo won his second 250cc world championship on Guzzi's 'Gambalunghino' (Little long-leg) single.

Norton Model 7

T he Dominator Model 7 was Norton's response to the Triumph Speed Twin, whose 500cc parallel twin engine had revolutionised motorcycling following its launch in 1937. Norton took some time to board the parallel-twin bandwagon, for chief designer Bert Hopwood did not start work until 1947. He aimed to create a powerplant that was stronger, quieter and less prone to overheating than Triumph's twin, and which could be produced using Norton's existing machinery.

Hopwood's Model 7, released two years later, gained its 497cc capacity from relatively short-stroke dimensions of 66 x 73mm. Unlike Triumph's motor, which had two gear-driven camshafts, the Norton used a single cam, situated at the front of the motor and driven by chain. Peak output was a respectable 29bhp, sufficient for a top speed of 90mph (145km/h).

One of Hopwood's design tasks had been ensuring that the Model 7's twin-cylinder motor was compact enough to fit into the chassis from the single-cylinder ES2. The single-downtube frame incorporated plunger rear suspension and Norton's Roadholder forks, which helped give the Model 7 stable and reliable handling with reasonable comfort.

Norton's introduction of the sportier, Featherbed-framed Dominator 88 in 1953 allowed the Model 7 to be repositioned as a less glamorous alternative. It was often fitted with a sidecar, and was popular as a flexible, reliable and stable roadster. It remained in Norton's range until 1956, gaining a larger front brake, alloy cylinder head and other updates along the way, before being replaced by the 600cc Model 77.

Above: *This 1952 vintage Model 7 is fitted with the chromed headlamp peak and crashbars that were popular accessories. Its original sprung saddle has also been replaced with the dual seat that Norton introduced as standard fitment for the following year.*

Norton Model 7 (1952)	
Engine Air-cooled ohv pushrod four-valve parallel twin	
Capacity 497cc (66 x 73mm)	
Maximum power 29bhp @ 7000rpm	
Transmission Four-speed, chain final drive	
Frame Steel single downtube	
Suspension Roadholder telescopic front; plunger rear	
Brakes Drum front & rear	
Weight 420lb (191kg)	
Top speed 90mph (145km/h)	

Indian Chief

he Chief led Indian's V-twin family for more than three decades, and remains an iconic machine due mainly to the unique style of later models. The 'Indian head' running light on a huge, skirted front mudguard reflected the character of the big, softly tuned, heavy and relatively low-tech Chief of the 1940s and early '50s; a bike that made up in style, comfort and cruising ability what it lacked in speed or handling prowess.

That late Chief's personality was very different to that of the original model, which was a much more performance-oriented machine. When Irish-born designer Charles B Franklin's initial Chief was launched in 1922, it used a frame based on that of the previous year's Scout model to hold a larger 998cc, side-valve V-twin engine developed from that of the long-running Powerplus. The Chief combined lively performance with good handling, but even so Indian promptly enlarged its engine to 1213cc (74ci) for the following year.

The so-called 'Big Chief' was a fine machine, its 40bhp output giving a top speed of 85mph (137km/h) in standard form. If featured leaf-spring front suspension, although a front brake was not added until 1928. By 1935 the Chief was available with the optional Y motor, which was more efficiently cooled due to its larger fins and aluminium instead of steel cylinder heads. The high-performance B or Bonneville powerplant, another option, incorporated hot cams, polished ports and precision timing, giving a top speed of 105mph (169km/h) that made the Chief one of the fastest bikes on the road.

Above: The late-model Chief's windscreen, running lights and crash-bars were all useful accessories but added to the big V-twin's already substantial weight.

Left: Huge skirted mudguards, tassels and an Indian's head light up front combined with the big V-twin engine to make the Chief instantly recognisable.

Indian struggled through the Depression of the 1930s, and lost ground to main rival Harley-Davidson, partly through its failure to introduce an overhead-valve replacement for the Chief's ageing side-valve powerplant. The Chief's emphasis on style was highlighted by the huge range of 24 standard paint schemes that were available, along with even more options at extra cost, after Indian had been taken over by the Du Pont chemical giant, which also produced paint.

The Chief was updated on numerous occasions, notably when being given the distinctive skirted mudguards in 1940, along with an uprated and cooler-running engine plus a new frame with plunger rear suspension. Girder forks had replaced the leaf-spring originals after World War II, and were in turn replaced by telescopics in 1950. At that time the engine was enlarged to 1311cc (80ci) by increasing its stroke to a huge 122mm, and Indian finally came into line with the rest of motorcycling by moving the hand-shift to the left side, and the throttle to the right.

The Chief of the early 1950s was stylish and comfortable, with those big mudguards, balloon tyres, a big 'buddy seat', and often an optional screen and leather panniers. But with a slow-revving 50bhp engine, standard three-speed box and over 550lb (250kg) of weight, it was not notably quick or agile. More importantly, sales were poor and Indian's financial problems had deepened following a failed attempt to sell small-capacity bikes. The last Chief left Indian's famous Springfield factory in 1953. Although the Indian name continued to be used on smaller bikes for some time, a big part of the US motorcycle scene had died.

Above: *Towards the end of its life the Chief was not particularly fast but it was stylish, comfortable and capable of effortless long-distance cruising.*

Indian Chief (1953)	
Engine Air-cooled four-valve side-valve 42-degree V-twin	
Capacity 1311cc (82.6 x 122mm)	
Maximum power 50bhp @ 4800rpm	
Transmission Three-speed, chain final drive	
Frame Steel twin downtube	
Suspension Telescopic front; plunger rear	
Brakes Drum front & rear	
Weight 570lb (259kg)	
Top speed 90mph (145km/h)	

AJS Model 16MCS

AJS was best known for its road-race bikes such as the 500cc Porcupine and the 350cc 7R 'Boy Racer'. But the firm also produced successful off-road competition machines in the 1950s, when even specialised trials bikes such as the Model 16MCS were closely related to roadgoing models.

In fact the 350cc, single-cylinder Model 16MCS was very similar not only to AJS's own Model 16 roadster but also to the Matchless G3. After Wolverhampton-based AJS was taken over by Matchless to create Associated Motor Cycles (AMC) in the 1930s, near-identical machines were produced under both marques' names, in the British bike industry's most blatant case of badge engineering.

AJS was the marque associated with off-road competition. Its works riders Hugh Viney and Gordon Jackson each won the prestigious Scottish Six-Day Trial six times during the 1950s and early '60s. The Model 16MCS was unofficially known as a 'Gordon Jackson Replica' although its differences from the standard Model 16 roadster amounted to little more than a smaller fuel tank, cut-down mudguards and a higher exhaust pipe.

The 347cc pushrod single engine produced a claimed 18bhp, enough to allow 60mph (97km/h) cruising, as well as the lively low-rev response that was useful off-road. The light weight of 330lb (150kg) contributed to the single's agile handling, and helped give reasonably lively acceleration. Performance was improved in 1960 when AJS updated the Model 16 with a 23bhp short-stroke motor. But in 1967 parent company AMC was taken over by Norton Villiers, which abandoned use of the AJS marque.

Above: This MCS engine's enclosed pushrod tubes reveal it is the revvier short-stroke unit, as favoured by trials ace Gordon Jackson.

Below: The MCS was a successful trials machine in 1954, but was very similar in most respects to AJS's Model 16 roadster – as well as sister firm Matchless's G3.

Moto Rumi 125 Sport

Above: *Like most of the bikes that Moto Rumi built, this stylish little 1954-model 125 Sport is powered by a two-stroke parallel-twin engine with horizontal cylinders.*

Rumi was an Italian marque that dared to be different. In an industry dominated by four-stroke singles from Guzzi and Gilera, the firm from Bergamo stood out with its distinctive machines, powered by 125cc two-stroke parallel twins with cylinders arranged horizontally, pointing forward. The marque's first bikes were launched in 1950. The Sport and Touring models shared many components, the most obvious difference between the two bikes being that the Turismo was more comprehensively equipped with larger mudguards and a more comfortable pillion seat.

The Sport, in particular, was a lean and handsome little machine. Its engine had different porting, pistons that gave a slightly higher compression ratio, and extra cooling fins on its barrels. Peak output was 8.5bhp at 6500rpm, good enough for a maximum speed of just over 60mph (97km/h). Another distinctive Rumi feature was the frame, which consisted of a steel 'double triangle' shape, with two pairs of tubes running diagonally from the cylinder head area at slightly different angles. The Sport's weight of just 198lb (90kg) helped give excellent handling.

Rumi expanded the two-stroke twin series with several other models during the 1950s, notably a Lusso ('Luxury') that was pitched mid-way between the Sport and Turismo. There was also a Bicarburatore (Twin-carburettor) version of the Sport, a high-performance Junior model with a new frame, and a scooter called the Formichino. The marque's founder Donnino Rumi also branched out with a series of four-stroke V-twins, but these were never produced in any volume, and Rumi's motorcycle business ceased in the 1960s.

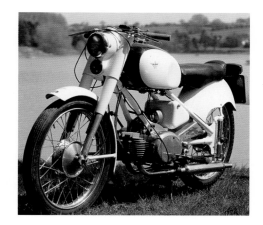

Above: *The Sport's telescopic forks combined with plunger rear suspension and the bike's light weight to give superbly agile handling.*

Triumph Tiger 100

Triumph's Tiger 100 was the hotted-up sports version of the Speed Twin whose parallel-twin engine had revolutionised motorcycling. That made it one of the fastest and best bikes of the late 1940s and early '50s. In standard form the Tiger 100 couldn't quite manage the 100mph (161km/h) speed that its name suggested, but its performance, smoothness and eye-catching silver paint scheme made it a hugely popular machine.

Paintwork apart, the Tiger 100 differed from the standard T5 Speed Twin in its higher, 7.8:1 compression ratio, which increased peak power output by 3bhp to 30bhp at 6500rpm. The 499cc pushrod parallel-twin engine was further uprated with an alloy top end in 1951, by which time the chassis had also been modified, with telescopic forks in place of the original girders.

In the mid-1950s Triumph improved the chassis again, this time at the rear with twin-shock suspension in place of the original sprung hub design. The updates kept the T100 competitive in the bends as well as on the straights, even if its handling was not quite up to Norton Featherbed standards.

By the late 1950s, when the basic Tiger had gained power with engine mods including sportier cams, it managed a genuine 105mph (169km/h). In 1960 it was replaced by an all-new model of the same name, complete with unit-construction engine and a revised chassis with bathtub rear enclosure. The 500cc twin remained in production throughout the decade, and in 1967 formed the basis of the twin-carburettor T100T Daytona.

Above: Triumph's typically lean styling combined with silver paintwork to make the Tiger 100 a very stylish machine, but it was the twin's lively performance that did most to make it popular.

Below: The Tiger's fairly flat, pulled-back handlebars allowed its rider to crouch forward and make the most of its acceleration and near-100mph (161km/h) top speed.

Velocette MAC

Velocette is best known for its TT-winning overhead-cam racebikes of the 1920s and '30s, and for the rapid Venom Thruxton of the 1960s. But it was the less glamorous MAC that epitomised the Birmingham marque's appeal. Quick, smooth, reliable, agile and competitively priced, it was everything a 350cc single-cylinder roadster should be.

Those racing 'cammy' singles such as the KTT earned Velocette a fine reputation for performance, but were expensive to produce and not very profitable. In 1933 the firm released the MOV ('OV' standing for 'Overhead Valve'), a simpler 250cc pushrod single. A year later its engine was enlarged to 349cc to create the 349cc MAC, which shared its styling with the smaller bike but added a fishtail silencer.

Velocette's steady development of the MAC included the adoption of telescopic forks in 1948, and a new aluminium cylinder and head in 1951. The 15bhp peak output gave a top speed of just over 70mph (113km/h). In 1953 the MAC was updated with a new twin-shock frame, which was heavier but gave the bike a new lease of life.

The MAC was a very capable performer by 1950s standards, which helped ensure its success, despite being more expensive than rival singles. It survived until the end of that decade with few further changes, but in 1960 was dropped from the range in favour of the sportier 350cc Viper. By that time the MAC had been in production for a quarter of a century, and had become Velocette's longest-running and best-selling model.

Above: Black paintwork, single-pot motor and big fishtail silencer were trademark Velocette features.

Velocette MAC (1954)

Engine Air-cooled ohv 2-valve pushrod single

Capacity 349cc (68 x 96mm)

Maximum power 15bhp @ 5000rpm

Transmission Four-speed, chain final drive

Frame Steel single downtube

Suspension Telescopic front; twin shocks rear

Brakes Drum front & rear

Weight 354lb (161kg)

Top speed 75mph (121km/h)

Douglas Dragonfly

The last and most stylish of the series of 348cc transverse flat twins produced by Bristol firm Douglas was the Dragonfly. With its distinctive headlamp nacelle blending into a large, rounded fuel tank, the Dragonfly made a big impact when launched at London's Earls Court Show in 1954. The sheet steel nacelle held the speedometer, a smaller ammeter and the ignition switch, as well as the headlamp.

The Dragonfly's engine retained Douglas's traditional capacity and chain final drive (in contrast to the shaft of BMW's boxers), but incorporated modifications including a stronger bottom-end and improved lubrication. The twin-downtube frame and the front suspension were built by chassis specialist Reynolds. The front suspension system, as fitted to BMWs, was the pivoted, twin-shock system designed by Ernie Earles, who had also styled the Dragonfly's nacelle. At the rear, twin shocks replaced Douglas's previous torsion bar suspension system. That combination gave the Dragonfly good handling as well as a pleasantly comfortable ride.

But the Dragonfly's straight-line performance was disappointing, as the bike was slightly slower than its predecessor the T35. Although its 17bhp engine allowed smooth cruising at 50mph (80km/h), and the four-speed gearbox was a big improvement, the bike lacked low-rev acceleration and its top speed was only just above 70mph (113km/h). Weak brakes, a high price and Douglas's reputation for poor reliability and quality control ensured that the Dragonfly wasn't the success that financially struggling Douglas needed, and it could not prevent the firm from going out of business in 1957.

Above: The Dragonfly's integrated headlamp nacelle and fuel tank helped make the boxer a very stylish machine. Earles forks added a further distinctive touch.

Below: Douglas's flat twin was a neat looking engine, but its modest output and reputation for unreliability condemned the Dragonfly to failure.

Ariel Red Hunter

Above and below: The Red Hunter 350 of 1956
was a solid, reliable machine, its character set by
its slow-revving 18bhp pushrod engine.

Ariel's Red Hunter is fondly remembered as one of the most dependable of 1950s motorbikes, if not one of the most exciting. The single-cylinder Hunter didn't approach the glamour of bikes including Ariel's own Square Four, but the single was a successful and long-lived model that remained in production for a quarter of a century.

Its origins were relatively sporty, for the Ariel singles of the 1920s were high-specification machines with four-valve cylinder heads. Although the NH350 Red Hunter and its big brother the VH500, which appeared in 1933, had two-valve heads, they were competitive in trials, scrambling and road-racing. The single was also converted to form the W/NG military model that was successfully used in World War II.

After the War, Ariel updated the Red Hunter with telescopic instead of girder forks. A further handling improvement came in 1954, with the adoption of a swing-arm chassis. By 1956 the bike's styling had evolved to include a headlamp nacelle and chromed fuel tank, and the engine had been updated with an alloy cylinder head. But the long-stroke Hunter motor still produced only 18bhp, enough to send it rumbling to just over 70mph (113km/h).

Despite that modest performance, the Hunter remained popular with riders impressed by its competitive price, economy, excellent finish (including features such as the fully-enclosed chaincase) and reliability. But as the 1960s approached, the days of the traditional British single were coming to an end. In 1958 Ariel abandoned production of its four-stroke roadsters, including the Red Hunter.

BSA Gold Star DBD34 Clubman

The lean, racy Gold Star Clubman was the ultimate street-legal competition bike of the 1950s. With its clip-on bars, chrome-panelled petrol tank, swept-back exhaust pipe and most of all its tuned 499cc single-cylinder powerplant, the 'Goldie' was fast, demanding and hugely popular – both with racers and with the road riders who valued its purposeful looks and thunderous 110mph (177km/h) performance.

Even the Gold Star's name was suitably evocative, for it referred to the lapel badge awarded to riders who lapped the banked Brooklands track at over 100mph (161km/h). The Gold Star model dated back to 1937, when BSA racer Wal Handley had earned the much-prized badge aboard the Birmingham firm's 500cc Empire Star.

The next year BSA released an uprated replica that it named the Gold Star in honour of Handley's lap. It featured a hotted-up engine incorporating an aluminium cylinder head and barrel, hand-polished inlet and exhaust ports,

Above: High-speed cornering was one of the Clubman Goldie's many strengths, thanks to its light weight, racy steering geometry and high quality suspension.

magnesium gearbox castings and other specially selected components. Peak power output was 28bhp, confirmed by the dyno chart that was issued with each machine. Despite having a relatively standard chassis for reasons of cost, the Gold Star handled very well and soon became popular.

One of the Goldie's greatest assets was its versatility. By 1950, BSA had introduced new versions of the single in 500cc ZB34 and 350cc ZB32 forms, both of which were competitive both on- and off-road. Their numerous factory options included four camshafts, four compression ratios (for use with different fuels from petrol to alcohol), and three alternative sets of gears: standard, road-racing or scrambling. Customers also had a choice of fuel tanks, exhaust systems and wheels.

In road-racing, in particular, the Gold Star built up a fearsome reputation. It dominated Clubman's (amateur) events at the Isle of Man TT, in both 500cc and 350cc classes. In the 1955 Junior TT, 33 of the 37 entrants were on Gold Stars, which led to the race being dropped from the programme after the following year.

The most famous Gold Star was the DBD34, which was launched in 1956, benefiting from BSA's development programme throughout the decade. Factory stars including Bill Nicholson had ridden Goldies to many wins in scrambles and trials, and introduced modifications including steeper steering geometry, swing-arm rear suspension (instead of plunger) and an improved front brake, which were incorporated into the production machine.

BSA's chief designer Bert Hopwood had also uprated the single-cylinder engine, notably two years earlier with the CB32 and CB34 models whose new top-ends had large finned cylinders. The DBD34 incorporated further improvements including a shorter, swept-back exhaust pipe, bigger Amal GP carburettor, and a close-ratio, four-speed gearbox that allowed a speed of almost 90mph (145km/h) in second.

In its classical, clip-on handlebarred Clubman form the Goldie was uncompromising and temperamental: often difficult to start, and too tall-geared and uncomfortable for slow-speed use. But the faster it went, the better it felt, and the uniquely single-minded BSA was much valued for its racetrack competitiveness and pure-bred roadgoing thrills alike. It remained in production until 1963.

Above: The famous Gold Star tank badge was inspired by racer Wal Handley's 'ton-up' lap of Brooklands in 1937.

Above left: The classical Gold Star look included chrome-flanked fuel tank, big front drum brake, heavily finned single-pot motor, unfiltered carburettor and swept-back exhaust.

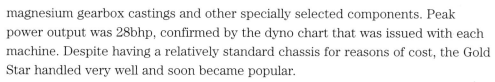

BSA DBD34 Gold Star Clubman (1956)	
Engine	Air-cooled ohv two-valve pushrod single
Capacity	499cc (85 x 88mm)
Maximum power	42bhp @ 7000rpm
Transmission	Four-speed, chain final drive
Frame	Steel twin downtube
Suspension	Telescopic front; twin shocks rear
Brakes	Drum front & rear
Weight	384lb (174kg)
Top speed	110mph (177km/h)

Sunbeam S8

The S8 was an attempt to go back to basics for Sunbeam, following the mechanical problems and poor sales of its controversial predecessor the S7. When the S8 was launched in 1949, its traditional black paintwork, slim look, conventional telescopic forks and narrow tyres were all in contrast to the bulkier S7, which had arrived two years earlier with unusual mist-green paintwork, innovative front forks and huge balloon tyres.

At heart the S8 was very similar to its imaginative but flawed forebear, for it shared the S7's 487cc tandem twin-cylinder engine layout and twin-downtube frame design. But the powerplant used higher compression ratio and a freer-breathing exhaust to increase peak output slightly to 26bhp, and more importantly was made more reliable by modifications including new pistons and extra oil capacity. And the chassis was improved by its use of BSA forks in place of the S7's undamped and poor-performing units, plus a revised rubber-mounting system that more efficiently isolated the twin-cylinder unit's vibration.

Performance was more lively than that of the S7. At 400lb (182kg) the S8 was substantially lighter, and it accelerated enthusiastically towards a top speed of just over 80mph (130km/h). The newer model handled better, too, and its engine proved reliable as well as smooth and easy to start. The S8 was also cheaper than the uprated S7 De Luxe that was introduced at the same time. But although the S8 sold reasonably well, all Sunbeam production was stopped following parent company BSA's merger with Triumph in 1956.

Sunbeam S8 (1949)	
Engine	Air-cooled sohc four-valve tandem twin
Capacity	487cc (70 x 63.5mm)
Maximum power	26bhp @ 5800rpm
Transmission	Four-speed, shaft final drive
Frame	Steel twin downtube
Suspension	Telescopic front; plunger rear
Brakes	Drum front & rear
Weight	400lb (182kg)
Top speed	82mph (132km/h)

Below: The S8's tandem twin powerplant was the S7's 487cc unit, strengthened and tuned with a higher compression ratio and a less restrictive exhaust system.

Left: The S8 was a much more conventional looking bike than the S7, and its reduced weight helped both acceleration and handling.

BSA Road Rocket

Above: *This 1957-model Road Rocket is a UK market machine, with lower bars and more restrictive pipes than the otherwise identical twins that BSA built for the US.*

Above: *For many riders in the US, the Road Rocket's 646cc capacity was as important a draw as its acceleration and top speed of over 100mph (161km/h).*

Three key ingredients for a successful bike in the US of the mid-1950s were style, performance and engine capacity. BSA's powerful and good-looking 650cc Road Rocket, launched in the States in 1954, provided plenty of all three. It became a big hit that did much to boost the Birmingham marque's fortunes in its most important market.

The Road Rocket was essentially a combination of a 646cc parallel-twin engine, based on that of BSA's recently released A10 Super Flash, and a new twin-shock chassis developed from that of the plunger-framed Golden Flash. The powerplant was tuned with an Amal TT9 carburettor, aluminium cylinder head, a hot camshaft, high-compression pistons, and toughened crankshaft.

The engine produced a maximum of 40bhp and was impressively flexible, giving thrilling acceleration, a claimed top speed of 105mph (169km/h) and a genuine cruising speed of over 90mph (145km/h). With its red paintwork and partly-chromed gas tank the Road Rocket was an eye-catching machine, and its chassis gave very reliable handling and braking. Despite its relatively high level of tune the motor proved impressively reliable, too.

The Rocket sold well in the States, and was also briefly popular on the UK home market, after being belatedly released in 1956. A year later it was succeeded by the Super Rocket, which featured a headlamp nacelle and redesigned cylinder head, but offered a similarly appealing blend of looks, speed and capacity. BSA's designers had discovered a successful formula, and were happy to keep on providing it.

Harley-Davidson Sportster

On its introduction in 1957, Harley-Davidson's Sportster justified its name with performance that made it one of the fastest and hardest-accelerating bikes on the road. The original Sportster was notable for its overhead valve operation, replacing the side-valve layout of Harley's existing 883cc K-series V-twin. Other features included short-stroke engine dimensions and bigger valves, which helped give a 40bhp peak output and a top speed of over 100mph (161km/h).

The Harley was a stylish machine, too, with two-tone paintwork, chrome-covered rear shocks, and the 'Sportster' name cast into its engine's primary drive cover. Frame and cycle parts came from its K-series predecessor, and gave respectably good handling and braking. It was as well built as it was fast, and quickly became popular, selling almost twice as many units in 1957 as the Model K had the previous year. As an alternative to its standard form, it could be adapted with accessories including windscreen, crash bars, luggage rack and panniers.

Harley introduced numerous Sportster variants in subsequent years, some incorporating a diminutive peanut fuel tank originally fitted to the firm's 125cc Hummer two-stroke. There was the off-road XLC, stripped of lights and with open pipes; and the XLH with its hotted-up engine. Fastest of all was the XLCH: originally a California-only dirtbike with tuned motor and no lights, before in 1959 being adapted to create a street-legal machine. Its style, performance and engaging V-twin character highlighted the raw appeal that would make the Sportster a long-lived legend.

Above: *The Sportster's 883cc overhead-valve V-twin engine gave straight-line performance that few 1957 rivals could match.*

Below: *Chrome-covered rear shocks, two-tone paintwork and the Sportster name cast into its engine cover all added to the Harley's undeniable visual appeal.*

Velocette LE

Velocette's LE or 'Little Engine' caused a sensation when unveiled at the London Motorcycle Show in 1948. The Birmingham marque was known for sporty big singles, but the LE was completely different to anything that Velocette or any other firm had built before.

Below its angular, pressed-steel monocoque frame was a liquid-cooled, four-stroke flat-twin engine of 149cc, its cylinders placed horizontally. The side-valve unit's maximum output was just 6bhp. Starting was by a long, hand-operated lever on the right of the bike; the gearbox was a three-speeder with a hand change.

The LE was an imaginative attempt at providing civilised commuting, and in many ways it was clever. Its monocoque frame helped keep dirt away from the rider; its legshields, footboards and large mudguards gave protection against weather; its liquid-cooled, shaft-drive engine was efficient and clean; and it had a useful pair of panniers.

Performance was reasonable by commuter bike standards but the LE was hindered by its strange styling, high price, and motorcyclists' distrust of an all-new model. Velo boss Eugene Goodman had budgeted to sell 14,500 units in 1950, so the final production total of just 2,800 was a disaster.

Velocette struggled on, updating the LE with numerous improvements in MkII and MkIII variants, the former launched in 1951 with a 192cc engine producing 8bhp. The public remained unconvinced. Approximately half of all the 33,000 LEs built during a period of 20 years were sold to the police forces, which valued its quietness and reliability.

Above: *The LE's curious look was based on its pressed-steel monocoque frame, below which sat a four-stroke flat-twin engine. Like many LEs, this 1957-model bike was initially used as a police bike.*

Above: *For a commuter machine the LE handled well, its stability enhanced by good quality suspension and large wheels.*

Triumph Thunderbird 650

Triumph's Thunderbird was made famous when ridden by Marlon Brando's character, Johnny, in the 1953 movie *The Wild One*. The hard-riding, hard-fighting Johnny struck a chord with many motorcyclists, and Triumph's fast and stylish machine was the perfect accomplice – especially as at the Thunderbird, with its new 649cc engine, had been the most powerful and quickest parallel twin on the market when launched three years earlier.

By the time the movie was released the T-bird was already well on the way to becoming a rip-roaring success. Triumph boss Edward Turner had created the model largely to satisfy the desire for increased engine capacity and horsepower in the US market, by far his company's most important in the 1950s. The T-bird was basically a bigger-engined version of the Speed Twin, whose parallel twin-cylinder engine had transformed the two-wheeled scene since the bike's introduction in 1938.

Enlarging the pushrod-operated powerplant to 649cc gave a healthy increase of midrange torque and a peak output of 34bhp, 7bhp up on the Speed Twin's figure. This resulted in notably improved acceleration, because the Thunderbird weighed 385lb (175kg), so was barely heavier than the smaller-engined model.

Above: The T-bird was just one of many popular Triumph twins in the '50s.

Below: Handling of this 1956-model T-bird benefited from the telescopic forks and twin-shock frame that had been introduced two years earlier.

The new bike got off to a high-profile start at the banked circuit of Montlhéry, outside Paris. The first three bikes off the production line were ridden for 500 miles (805km) at an average speed of over 92mph (148km/h), with a last lap of over 100mph (161km/h). All three were standard apart from minor mods such as fitment of rearset footrests and racing tyres, so it was an impressive introduction.

The T-bird quickly become popular in both home and export markets, boosted by favourable press comments regarding its distance-covering ability. The Triumph cruised effortlessly at 60mph (97km/h), prompting *The Motor Cycle* magazine's tester to comment that its quietness and smoothness between that speed and 70mph (113km/h) were 'quite exceptional'. Two-way average speed, as tested by that magazine in 1950, was 97mph (156km/h), so the T-bird was just capable of genuine 'ton-up' performance.

Equally impressively, it proved reliable despite serious provocation. 'During the days when attempts were made to obtain the maximum speed figures, the engine took such a flogging as is unlikely ever to come the way of a machine in the hands of even the hardest of everyday riders,' the magazine's tester wrote. 'The engine was on full-bore almost continuously for three or four hours at a stretch on four consecutive days. It gave no signs of abuse.'

Handling was generally good, and got better still in the mid-1950s when Triumph introduced a new twin-shock frame, replacing the original model's option of hard-tail or sprung-hub rear suspension. The chassis was further improved in 1960, when the Thunderbird was also fitted with Triumph's controversial 'bathtub' enclosed rear end. By this time the arrival of the more powerful Tiger 110 had pushed the T-bird into a touring role. But the model's influence in helping establish Triumph in the US market, in particular, had made it one of the Meriden firm's most important models.

Above: The late-'50s Thunderbird was a strikingly lean and stylish machine with no sign of the controversial 'bathtub' bodywork that gave later models a less sporty image.

Triumph Thunderbird (1956)

Engine Air-cooled ohv four-valve pushrod parallel twin

Capacity 649cc (71 x 82mm)

Maximum power 34bhp @ 6300rpm

Transmission Four-speed, chain final drive

Frame Steel twin downtube

Suspension Telescopic front, twin shocks rear

Brakes Drum front and rear

Weight 396lb (180kg)

Top speed 97mph (156km/h)

Royal Enfield Constellation

The Constellation was one of a string of distinctive parallel twins built by Royal Enfield during the 1950s and '60s. Most had the unusual capacity of 692cc, which came about because in 1953 Enfield had created the Meteor twin by putting together a pair of 346cc engines from the Bullet single. The Constellation was launched two years later with a hotted-up motor incorporating new cams and cylinder heads, an increased compression ratio and an impressive peak output of 51bhp.

There was no doubting the Constellation's speed. One early magazine test recorded a two-way average of 112mph (179km/h), matching or beating rival twins. Acceleration was particularly strong, aided by the big motor's generous low-rev torque. The Enfield also handled well thanks to a chassis which, in Enfield tradition, used the engine as a stressed member of the frame.

But the Constellation's appeal was diminished by its unreliability. It ran well at relatively low revs, but when ridden hard the engine developed problems including oil leaks, blowing head gaskets and conrod failure. Enfield's development engineers did their best. During its five-year existence the Constellation gained engine updates including revised crankcase breathing, in an attempt to cure the leaks, and was also fitted with low Ace handlebars.

By 1963, the Constellation's last year before its motor was enlarged to produce the Interceptor 750, Enfield had introduced further modifications including reduced compression and a rebalanced crankshaft, which did much to improve reliability. But the public remained unconvinced, and production of all Enfield's quirky twins ended in 1970.

Above: The late-model Constellation's low bars encouraged its rider to crouch low and let the big twin show its impressive straight-line speed.

Below: This Constellation was built in 1963 so incorporates the reduced compression ratio and rebalanced crankshaft that improved the big twin but did not totally cure its problems or make it a sales success.

Harley-Davidson Duo-Glide

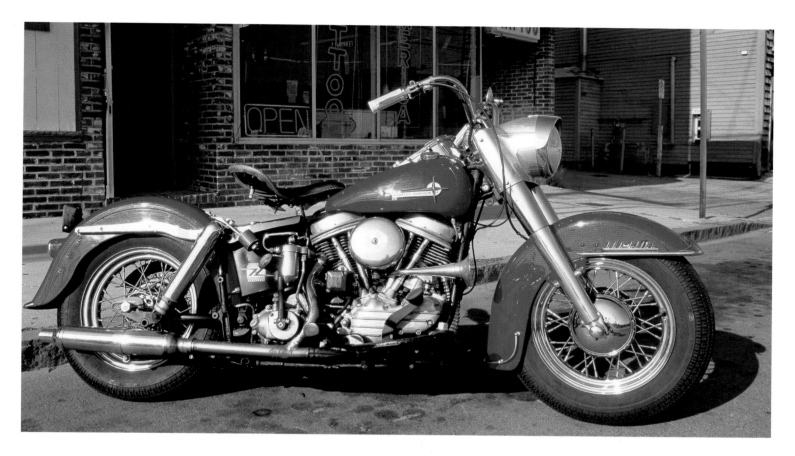

Harley-Davidson faced tough competition from lighter British parallel twins in the 1950s. The firm responded by improving its large-capacity V-twins – known as 'Panheads' after the shape of their cylinder heads – with a series of features that improved functionality while leaving the look and character unchanged. One of the most significant was the 1958-model Duo-Glide, whose name – picked out in chromed lettering on the front mudguard for the first time – announced that this bike had suspension at both ends, instead of just up front.

Harley had been slow to introduce hydraulic suspension, but had finally done so in 1950 with the Hydra-Glide, a name that referred to the EL model's new hydraulically damped telescopic front fork, but which came to represent the bike itself. As well as a smoother ride, the fork gave a cleaner look in conjunction with larger mudguards. The FLH Duo-Glide was another advance. It added features including a hydraulic rear brake and optional whitewall tyres, as well as the chrome-covered, hydraulically damped shocks that gave the bike its name.

The Duo-Glide's 1208cc (74ci) V-twin engine produced a claimed maximum of 52bhp, good for a top speed of 100mph (161km/h). The bike was an impressively comfortable cruiser, especially when fitted with its optional windscreen. By 1958 Harley was the only significant US bike firm, following Indian's halt of V-twin production five years earlier. The Duo-Glide was an important step in the fightback against the British manufacturers that were targeting the US market with increasing success.

Above: Telescopic forks and chrome-covered rear shocks earned the Duo-Glide its name and gave a comfortable ride.

Harley-Davidson Duo-Glide (1958)	
Engine	Air-cooled ohv four-valve pushrod 45-degree V-twin
Capacity	1208cc (87 x 101mm)
Maximum power	52bhp @ 5000rpm
Transmission	Four-speed, chain final drive
Frame	Tubular steel
Suspension	Telescopic front; twin shocks rear
Brakes	Drum front & rear
Weight	648lb (294kg)
Top speed	100mph (161km/h)

Norton Dominator 88

otorcycling's best known frame design is the Norton Featherbed, the brilliantly simple and stiff twin-loop steel cradle that earned its name when works rider Harold Daniell commented that his newly upgraded racebike was so comfortable it was like 'riding a feather bed'. The Featherbed was introduced on Norton's single-cylinder Manx racers in 1950, and two years later was adapted to house the twin-cylinder roadgoing powerplant of the new Dominator 88.

Norton's 497cc pushrod twin-cylinder unit had made its debut in the 1949-model Dominator Model 7, and fitted easily into the Featherbed frame. The Irish racing brothers Rex and Cromie McCandless, the frame's creators, had designed it to be capable of housing a wide variety of Norton engines and gearboxes. Just as with the Manx racer, the twin-shock frame gave the Dominator not just more comfort but also significantly improved handling and roadholding.

The Dominator 88 was also lighter than its predecessor, at 405lb (184kg), which helped give it a more sporty nature as it roared towards a top speed of over 90mph (145km/h). The model gained some extra performance in 1955, with the introduction of an aluminium cylinder head, plus increased compression and an Amal Monobloc carburettor. Even so, the Norton was slightly slower than its Triumph and BSA rivals in a straight line. But the superb handling provided by that Featherbed frame ensured that provided there were plenty of bends in the road, a Dominator 88 rider had every chance of being at the front of the pack.

Above: Its Featherbed frame gave the Dominator excellent high-speed stability as well as impressive cornering performance.

Below: This late-model Dominator 88 incorporates the alloy cylinder head, higher compression ratio and slimline Featherbed frame that made Norton's twin faster and more manageable.

Honda C71

Honda's well-built and reliable small-capacity models, led by the C71, heralded a new motorcycling era when they reached Europe and the United States in the late 1950s. The C71 and its Japanese-market-only predecessor the C70 were inspired by German firm NSU's rapid Rennmax twin-cylinder racers, which had impressed Soichiro Honda on his visit to Europe a few years earlier. Honda's 247cc engine used a single overhead camshaft, unlike the dohc NSUs. It produced 18bhp and featured an electric starter.

The name on the partly-chromed tank was Dream, which Honda had used ever since his firm's first wholly built machine, the 98cc Model D of 1949. The frame, front forks and swing-arm were made from pressed-steel sections, which had the advantage of being quick and inexpensive to produce. The forks were short, leading-link units with spring and damper units inside the pressings. The rear shock units were rectangular in section and, along with the huge mudguards, contributed to the bike's old-fashioned appearance.

Although the C71 was no sports bike it had very acceptable performance, with a top speed of 80mph (129km/h). The soft and simple suspension gave mediocre handling but the Honda's brakes were impressive. So were features including its indicators, comprehensive tool kit, reliability and ease of maintenance. The twin was a high-quality package, albeit an expensive one by 250cc standards. Few were sold in the West, but with the C71 and its contemporaries Honda laid the foundations for Japan's future motorcycling dominance.

Honda C71 (1960)	
Engine	Air-cooled sohc four-valve parallel twin
Capacity	247cc (54 x 54mm)
Maximum power	18bhp @ 7400rpm
Transmission	Four-speed, chain final drive
Frame	Pressed-steel spine
Suspension	Leading-link front; twin shocks rear
Brakes	Drum front & rear
Weight	354lb (161kg)
Top speed	80mph (129km/h)

Above: The C71 was solidly engineered and performed quite well but its old-fashioned look did not increase Honda's chance of success in export markets.

Left: Like its frame and swing-arm, the Honda's leading-axle front forks were made from pressed steel, which was cheap to produce but provided neither style not optimum performance.

BSA A10 Golden Flash

Motorcycle firms normally attempt to avoid rushing development of a new model, as this is likely to lead to problems. BSA's A10 proved a notable exception to that rule. In 1949, BSA's management decided the firm needed a 650cc model, and gave recently appointed designer Bert Hopwood just four weeks to create a new powerplant based on the 499cc A7. The A10 Golden Flash was designed, tested and in production by November of the same year. Despite the rush, the Golden Flash proved reliable and became a long-lasting success for the Birmingham firm.

BSA's 646cc engine differed from Triumph's parallel-twin unit by having a single, four-lobe camshaft instead of twin cams. The A10 produced a maximum of 35bhp, and was reasonably smooth, torquey and reliable. Its chassis initially incorporated plunger rear suspension, with the option of a rigid frame for sidecar use. The more modern system of swing-arm and twin shock absorbers was introduced in 1954, when other changes to the Flash included revised front forks and a new gearbox.

Far from living up to its name by being a racy sportster, the Golden Flash was a dependable but not particularly exciting all-rounder that was at its best when lugging a sidecar. While BSA's sportier Gold Star single fought for the high-speed headlines with Triumph's Bonneville and Norton's Dominator twins, the Golden Flash's main attractions were its comfort and flexible power delivery. It remained in production through various updates until 1963, when the A10 was replaced by BSA's 'unit construction' A65 range, featuring combined engine and gearbox.

Above: BSA's 646cc A10 engine delivered good all-round performance and proved impressively reliable, despite its lack of development time.

Below: The later Golden Flash's twin-shock rear end improved handling, but did not change the model's image as a comfortable all-rounder with flexible power delivery.

Matchless G12

Above: Matchless fitted a new long-stroke crankshaft to give the G12's parallel-twin powerplant a capacity of 646cc.

Left: This 1959-model G12 De Luxe features the slim rear shocks that replaced the distinctively fat 'jampot' design in 1957, but not the twin-downtube frame that was introduced in 1960.

The Matchless G12, like its twin the AJS Model 31, was one of the more successful products of the badge engineering that saw near-identical machines marketed with different names following the merger that resulted in the formation of Associated Motor Cycles (AMC). Matchless, the old firm whose co-founder Charlie Collier had won the single-cylinder race at the first ever Isle of Man TT in 1907, had taken over AJS of Wolverhampton in 1931. Production continued at the Matchless factory in south London, and both marques' names continued to be used.

When the 646cc G12/Model 31 was introduced in 1959, it traced its lineage back ten years to the Matchless G9, a 498cc parallel twin also sold as the AJS Model 20. That was a flexible and sweet-running bike whose engine was bored out to 592cc in 1956, creating the G11/Model 30. The engine could not be bored out any further, so for the G12/Model 31 AMC developed a longer-stroke crankshaft that took capacity to 646cc.

The G12's additional capacity gave even more mid-range punch. The bike made a fairly popular all-rounder, thanks to its lively acceleration, impressive low-rev docility, and respectable top speed of just over 100mph (161km/h). It also handled well and was reliable, both in standard form or as the slightly more expensive De Luxe, which incorporated an uprated ignition and quickly-detachable rear wheel. Unfortunately the same could not be said of the hotted-up G12 CSR, which stormed to a top speed of 108mph (174km/h) but vibrated and frequently broke.

Matchless G12 De Luxe (1959)	
Engine Air-cooled ohv pushrod four-valve parallel twin	
Capacity 646cc (72 x 79.3mm)	
Maximum power 35bhp @ 6000rpm	
Transmission Four-speed, chain final drive	
Frame Steel single downtube	
Suspension Telescopic front; twin shocks rear	
Brakes Drum front & rear	
Weight 400lb (182kg)	
Top speed 102mph (164km/h)	

Triumph TR6 Trophy

With its neat styling, punchy parallel twin engine and high-level exhaust system, Triumph's TR6 Trophy was as cool as it was fast. When it was launched in 1956, the off-road oriented twin was arguably the first 'street scrambler' from a major manufacturer. It was built specifically for export; targeted not simply at the States but more precisely at California, where desert racing was hugely popular.

Triumph created the TR6 Trophy by fitting the existing 500cc TR5 Trophy with a 649cc engine, based on the unit that had made its debut in the Thunderbird roadster in 1950. The T-bird's lasting popularity led to the new TR6 Trophy being nicknamed the 'Trophy-bird' in the States. It was most popular with Californian based off-road enthusiasts including movie star Steve McQueen and his friend Bud Ekins, a scrambles ace who doubled for McQueen in some riding stunts in *The Great Escape*. The TR6 became regarded as the ideal 'desert sled' for charging through hot, desolate places such as the Mojave Desert.

Triumph's 42bhp twin-cylinder engine gave a top speed of over 100mph (161km/h) in standard tune, plus the mid-range punch to let the rider steer on the throttle on loose surfaces. Many competition riders made modifications including removing lights and exhaust baffles, and fitting a cut-down seat, off-road tyres and a metal bash-plate. Plenty of others were happy to keep the Trophy-bird relatively standard, enjoying the style and performance that made it one of the most successful bikes that Triumph ever built.

Above: *Triumph's 649cc parallel twin gave plenty of performance for both on- and off-road use.*

Below: *Its high-level exhaust made the TR6 better suited to off-road riding, and many owners modified the twin to make it faster, lighter and more robust.*

Panther Model 100

The Model 100 was the longest surviving and best known of Panther's 'sloper' singles, named after their single, angled-forward cylinder. It was introduced in 1928 and remained in production until 1963. The Model 100 name referred to the 100mm stroke of the 598cc single-pot engine.

Panther – or Phelon & Moore Ltd, as the company from Cleckheaton in Yorkshire was really called – had a long history of building motorbikes with a single sloping cylinder that also acted as the frame's downtube. P&M's first ever bike featured a 500cc engine with that layout in 1904, as did the very first prototype built by Joah Phelon, the firm's founder, in 1900.

The Model 100's peak power output never exceeded 23bhp, and top speed was a modest 70mph (112km/h). But the long-stroke pushrod single's low-rev torque and pair of big, heavy flywheels made the Panther well suited to pulling a sidecar in the 1940s and '50s, when an outfit was frequently the main method of family transport. In 1960 the firm estimated that 90 per cent of Model 100s were attached to sidecars.

By this time many motorcyclists with families were being tempted by small cars, and the days of the combination were numbered. P&M attempted to extend the single's life with the Model 120S, which featured an enlarged, 645cc engine that produced 27bhp. But its sales were not enough to prevent the Yorkshire firm hitting financial problems, and the factory closed in 1967. The Panther's departure confirmed the end of a motorcycling era.

Panther Model 100 (1957)	
Engine	Air-cooled ohv 2-valve single
Capacity	598cc (87 x 100mm)
Maximum power	23bhp @ 5300rpm
Transmission	Four-speed, chain final drive
Frame	Steel spine
Suspension	Telescopic front; twin shock rear
Brakes	Drum front & rear
Weight	425lb (193kg)
Top speed	70mph (112km/h)

Below: A high proportion of Panthers were used to pull sidecars but the late-model 'sloper' also made a dependable, if less than exciting, machine for solo use.

Chapter 3

The 1960s

Honda CB92

Honda's CB92 Benly Super Sport wasn't merely the fastest 125cc bike around in the early 1960s, it could also embarrass many much larger machines on both road and track. The CB92 was the sports version of Honda's C92 parallel twin. As well as being very quick for a 125cc machine, it was stylish, cleverly engineered and well equipped.

The CB92's angled-forward, sohc twin-cylinder engine layout was shared with the heavier and more angular roadster models with which Honda had made its initial attempt at export sales. But the Super Sport was notably more stylish, despite its rather dated pressed-steel frame and leading-link forks. Its featured a big front drum brake, low handlebars set behind a racy flyscreen, and a humped fuel tank with rubber pad at the rear.

The Honda's compact, air-cooled 124cc motor produced its maximum of 15bhp at a heady 10,500rpm. The motor had to be kept spinning at over 7000rpm to give of its best, and rewarded its rider's effort with genuine 75mph (121km/h) performance. Its suspension didn't match the quality of its engine but the lightweight Honda was nevertheless very agile.

The CB92's cornering and braking ability had much to do with its giant-killing performance. The little twin was also engineered to the high standard for which Honda, for whom Mike Hailwood and Australia's Tom Phillis won the 250 and 125cc World Championships in 1961, was becoming known. The little bike gained plenty of admirers and did much to boost Honda's reputation for performance and high technology.

Above: *With its rider's head tucked behind its tiny flyscreen, the CB92 was capable of a genuine 75mph (121km/h).*

Below: *The Honda's 124cc, sohc parallel twin produced a maximum of 15bhp and revved to 10,500rpm with impressive reliability.*

Left: *Despite its old-fashioned pressed steel frame and leading-link forks, the CB92 was a much sportier-looking machine than many of its Honda contemporaries from the early '60s.*

Moto Guzzi Falcone

T he Falcone was one of motorcycling's longest-lasting models, remaining in production for 18 years during the 1950s and '60s with few changes, before being revamped to return as the Falcone Nuovo (New Falcon) for a further eight years. Throughout that time it retained the classical Moto Guzzi single-cylinder engine layout – a 500cc horizontal pot with large external 'bacon-slicer' flywheel – which dated back to the Normale model with which Carlo Guzzi and Giorgio Parodi had begun the marque's production in 1921.

Guzzi's flat-singles had already established a strong reputation when the original Falcone was introduced in 1950, its design owing much to the Mandello marque's exotic road-racing machines – the Condor, Albatross and Dondolino. The Falcone was an attractive machine, with slim lines, bright red paintwork and a fairly sporty riding position thanks to low handlebars and a rear seat-pad that allowed the rider to get into a racing crouch. It produced 23bhp, was good for 80mph (130km/h), handled well, and was much cheaper than the Dondolino racer.

Most of the changes that Guzzi made to the Falcone over its long life were minor, the most significant coming when the original model became the Falcone Sport and a new, softer version, the Turismo, was introduced. Even after production ended in 1968, the single was redesigned and reintroduced as the Falcone Nuovo. That bike was introduced in 1969 mainly for police and military use, but civilian versions followed and the Falcone Nuovo was produced right up until 1976.

Above: This Falcone dates from 1964 and is the Turismo version, more common than the slightly more powerful Sport. The raised headlamp design was originally to allow room for a siren on police models.

Above: Guzzi's 498cc flat-single engine produced 19bhp in its Turismo specification – 4bhp down on the Sport due to reduced compression ratio and smaller Dell'Orto carburettor.

Triumph T120 Bonneville

Triumph created its most famous and popular model in 1959 by fitting the existing 649cc Tiger 110 with a new cylinder head and twin carburettors. The resultant sports roadster was named T120 after its supposed top speed, and Bonneville after the salt flats in Utah, where a streamlined Triumph ridden by Johnny Allen had been timed at 214mph (344km/h) three years earlier. The fast and stylish 'Bonnie' would be the star of Triumph's range for years to come.

The original T120 required relatively little development. Its format of 649cc parallel twin, with pushrod valve operation, four-speed gearbox and 360-degree crankshaft, was identical to that of the Tiger 110. Even the tuning components were familiar, because in 1958 the Tiger had been available with an optional cylinder head incorporating splayed inlet ports, for fitment of twin carburettors, plus a list of performance parts including hot cams and Amal racing carbs.

Above and below left: The T120 Bonnie's lean lines and rev-happy engine combined to make it one of the most popular bikes on the road throughout the '60s.

Triumph's US distributors had requested a high-performance model, so the Meriden firm created the T120 by incorporating the sportier head plus a pair of Amal Monobloc carbs as standard fitment. The new twin's claimed peak output of 46bhp was 4bhp up on that of the Tiger. For its 1959 debut the Bonneville, which was put together hurriedly and was not featured in that year's Triumph catalogue, retained the Tiger's headlamp nacelle and touring handlebars.

As well as having thrilling acceleration to a 110mph (176km/h) top speed, the Bonneville was reasonably smooth. But the original T120's engine performance occasionally overwhelmed its single-downtube frame, making the bike prone to high-speed instability. For 1960 Triumph introduced a new twin-cradle frame with steeper steering geometry and shorter wheelbase, plus new forks and sportier styling featuring a separate headlamp shell and smaller mudguards.

Following some frame-cracking problems the chassis was strengthened for 1961. Triumph updated the Bonnie regularly over the next decade and created several variations. The basic home-market T120 was joined by the T120C competition model and a stylish if less practical export version, featuring high handlebars and a small fuel tank. In 1963, the factory introduced a redesigned 'unit' 650 with engine and gearbox combined instead of the previous separate or pre-unit layout.

The Bonneville's handling was never as highly rated as that of its Norton rivals, but the Triumph's all-round performance was hard to beat. That was also true on a racetrack, including the Isle of Man. John Hartle won the production TT in 1967, and Malcolm Uphill repeated the feat two years later, setting the first production 100mph (160km/h) lap in the process. The T120 also took four wins in the prestigious 500-mile (805km) production races at Thruxton and Brands Hatch, with riders including Triumph's tester Percy Tait.

In 1971 the Bonnie was redesigned with a taller, so-called 'oil-in-frame' chassis, which was heavily criticised until hastily revised to lower the seat height. By 1972, Triumph had produced an estimated 250,000 Bonnevilles. The T120's reign ended the following year, when engine capacity was increased to 744cc, producing the torquier but less smooth-running T140 Bonneville.

Triumph T120 Bonneville (1961)	
Engine	Air-cooled four-valve ohv pushrod parallel twin
Capacity	649cc (71 x 82mm)
Maximum power	46bhp @ 6500rpm
Transmission	Four-speed, chain final drive
Frame	Steel twin downtube
Suspension	Telescopic front; twin shocks rear
Brakes	Drum front & rear
Weight	402lb (183kg) wet
Top speed	110mph (177km/h)

Below: The Bonneville's visual appeal matched its performance – which is boosted in this 1962-model's case by flat bars and filterless Amal carbs.

Norton 650SS Dominator

The sleek 650SS Dominator was Norton's finest parallel twin for much of the 1960s. Its flexible powerplant, refined character and especially the fine handling provided by Norton's Featherbed frame all combined to make the SS popular for much of the decade, without ever matching the sales success of rival Triumph twins such as the Bonneville.

Norton created the 650SS in 1962 by taking the firm's 646cc parallel-twin powerplant, released in the previous year's export-only Manxman 650, and adapting it with the tuning modifications – notably high compression pistons and twin carburettors – that had been developed for 500cc and 600cc twins under the name Sports Special or SS. The 650SS also incorporated a strengthened bottom-end design plus a downdraft cylinder head layout, with steeply angled Amal carburettors, developed from engineer Doug Hele's powerful Domiracer competition bike.

The 650SS motor produced 49bhp with plenty of midrange plus reasonable smoothness, and the bike's fine handling and braking made it an impressive all-round performer with a top speed of almost 120mph (193km/h). When Norton advertised it as 'the world's best road holder', few rival firms could disagree.

The SS was voted Motor Cycle News machine of the year in 1962 and '63, and won prestigious long-distance production races at Thruxton and Silverstone. The last bikes to be built at Norton's traditional base in Bracebridge Street, Birmingham, before its closure in 1963, were 650SS models for the Australian police. The twin remained in production for another five years at parent company AMC's factory in south London.

Above: Restrained styling only hinted at the performance of the 650SS, whose blend of power and fine handling resulted in one of the fastest bikes of the '60s.

Above: The 49bhp parallel twin engine was held by Norton's outstandingly rigid tubular-steel Featherbed frame.

Ariel Leader

Ariel Leader (1958)	
Engine Air-cooled two-stroke parallel twin	
Capacity 249cc (54 x 54mm)	
Maximum power 16bhp @ 6400rpm	
Transmission Four-speed, chain final drive	
Frame Pressed-steel backbone	
Suspension Trailing link telescopic front; twin shocks rear	
Brakes Drum front & rear	
Weight 310lb (141kg)	
Top speed 73mph (117km/h)	

Left: The Leader's large fairing, screen, big mudguards and panniers helped make it an outstandingly practical machine that coped well with adverse weather conditions.

When Ariel launched the fully enclosed Leader in 1958 it was a radical machine about which the firm's advertising slogan 'Tomorrow's Design Today' rang true. The Leader's weather protection and styling owed much to scooters, while its 250cc two-stroke parallel twin engine and its chassis gave the performance and handling of a motorcycle.

The Leader, along with the stripped-down Arrow derivative that followed two years later, was a bold attempt by Ariel, which was part of the BSA group, to provide a practical, easily maintained machine. Its 16bhp engine owed much to that of the German Adler. The frame was a pressed steel backbone, holding trailing-link forks. Further pressed-steel sections gave the Leader its unique appearance. The dummy fuel tank, complete with rubber kneegrips, could store an open-face helmet. The fairing was made from similar pressed steel and, with its leg shields and near-vertical screen, gave generous weather protection.

The Leader accelerated briskly and cruised reasonably smoothly at 55mph (89km/h), with a little in hand before its top speed of just over 70mph (113km/h). It handled quite well and was pleasantly light and agile. But the two-stroke engine were smoky and could be hard to start. Electrics were unreliable, and the gearbox caused problems.

After a promising start, sales declined rapidly. This was disastrous for Ariel, which had abandoned four-stroke manufacture in 1960. In 1965 production of both Leader and Arrow was halted. Parent company BSA had run out of patience with Ariel, whose great two-stroke gamble had failed.

Above: This 1962-model Leader benefited from the new cylinder head, introduced in the previous year, which increased peak power output from 16 to 17.5bhp.

Honda CB72

The fast and sporty CB72 did more than any other bike to improve the image of Japanese machines in the early 1960s. This 247cc four-stroke parallel twin was the model that proved Honda was getting serious. Until the CB72 reached export markets in 1962, Honda's roadsters had typically been well made but curiously styled and heavy. The new twin – known as the Dream Super Sport in Britain and the Hawk in the US – was very different.

The CB72 was the sporty version of Honda's three-model 250cc range. It had low handlebars, a thinly padded dual seat, and an innovative instrument panel incorporating speedometer and rev-counter whose needles rotated in opposite directions. Twin carbs helped give a peak output of 24bhp. The chassis changes were even more important. In place of a pressed-steel frame was a new and more rigid tubular construction, based on that of Honda's works racers. Traditional leading-link front suspension was replaced by telescopics, with a pair of round-section shocks at the rear.

Those features gave the CB72 a much more racy and modern look, and riding it did not disappoint. Top speed was a genuine 90mph (145km/h), with acceleration to match. The Honda was stable at speed, and handled well thanks to reasonably firm suspension. Its brakes, twin leading-shoe drums at each end, were powerful too. The CB72 impressed not only with its speed and chassis performance but also with its quality and reliability. It proved once and for all that Honda could made quick, fine-handling and stylish bikes.

Above: The Honda's sweet-revving and reliable 247cc parallel-twin engine used a single overhead camshaft to produce a maximum of 24bhp.

Below: The CB72's tubular-steel frame, telescopic forks and conventional rear shocks contrasted with the old-fashioned chassis design of previous Honda roadsters.

BSA Rocket Gold Star

BSA's A10 line of 'pre-unit' 646cc parallel twins ended in spectacular style with the Rocket Gold Star, which housed the powerful twin-pot motor from the Super Rocket in a high-quality chassis derived from that of the single-cylinder Gold Star. The factory RGS, launched in 1962, was inspired by a one-off special that Oxfordshire BSA dealer Eddie Dow had built for a customer. A few modifications were made for production, but the blend of top-class engine and chassis performance was very much intact.

The uprated engine incorporated an aluminium cylinder head with increased 9:1 compression ration, hotter camshaft, and racing-style magneto with manual advance-retard adjustment. Peak output was raised slightly to 46bhp, or 50bhp when fitted with the optional Gold Star style racing silencer. The chassis was of equally high specification, including Gold Star gaitered forks, large-capacity alloy fuel tank, close-ratio gearbox, siamesed exhaust system, humped racing seat, alloy wheel rims, and a big front drum brake.

The result was a stunningly purposeful machine that was one of the ultimate café racers. It roared to a genuine top speed of 115mph (145km/h), and was ideally suited to high-speed runs when in home-market specification with Gold Star style clip-on bars, instead of the higher bars fitted to export models. Handling and braking were also very highly rated. At the end of 1963, BSA halted production to concentrate on its new 654cc line of unit-construction twins. The Rocket Goldie had been a fine way for the A10 line to end.

Above: The rev-counter, on right, was an optional extra that was popular with many Rocket Gold Star riders, as were rearset footrests and alloy wheel rims.

Below: This 1963-model Rocket Goldie is an American-market machine, with higher bars and a smaller tank than the bikes built for the British café-racer crowd.

Yamaha YDS-2

The YDS-2 made a big contribution towards establishing not just Yamaha but small-capacity Japanese two-strokes in general as a popular form of transport. The little 250cc twin was rev-happy, loud, reasonably cheap and impressively reliable. Most of all, it was fast enough to outrun every 250cc rival following its arrival in export markets in 1962.

Parent company Nippon Gakki, best known for musical instruments, had turned to motorcycle production only in 1955 as a way of utilising machinery that had been used to make propellers in World War II. Yamaha's first models, such as the 125cc YA-1 or 'Red Dragonfly' single, and the 250cc YD-2, the firm's first twin, had confirmed the firm's expertise at building small-capacity two-strokes. But those bikes and sportier 250cc YDS1 had been sold mainly on the home market.

The YDS-2 changed all that. It was this lively little twin that began the Japanese firm's long run of success with small- and medium-capacity two-strokes. Its straight-line speed came from a simple air-cooled, piston-ported two-stroke parallel twin engine. Capacity was 246cc; claimed peak output was 25bhp at 7500rpm. A pair of Amal carburettors provided the fuel – a mixture of petrol and oil that, in old-fashioned style, had to be pre-mixed in the tank at every fill up.

Chassis layout was typical of the 1960s, with a steel twin-cradle frame, simple front forks, twin rear shocks and 18-inch wire-spoked wheels. Styling was neat

Above: The little Yamaha's agile handling was almost as vital to its appeal as its lively straight-line performance.

Below: The YDS-2's styling owed much to Yamahas of the late 1950s. The tuning fork tank badge was a reference to the firm's production of musical instruments.

and restrained, Yamaha's tuning-fork badges sharing space on the tank with rubber kneepads.

There was no doubting the YDS-2's ability to produce thrilling acceleration and the 90mph (145km/h) top speed claimed in contemporary adverts. The 180-degree-crankshaft motor was smooth, too, just about justifying the 'twin cylinder – smooth as a four' comment that came under the advertising headline 'Greatest Yamaha Ever Built'. Chassis performance was nowhere near as impressive as the engine, but the YDS-2's weight of just 312lb (142kg) helped make it agile, and its brakes were highly rated. Even its stability and general handling were praised in contemporary reports, despite soft and wallowy suspension that was described by US magazine Cycle World as 'too soft for anything but touring'.

Like the other Japanese manufacturers, Yamaha would take more than another ten years to get its machines' handling really sorted out. But it's a reflection of the firm's determination to improve its product that just a year later the YDS-2 was replaced by the YDS-3 – featuring not only an automatic Autolube engine lubrication system and a couple of extra horsepower, but also stiffer suspension at both front and rear.

Larger-capacity models followed, too, starting with the 305cc YM-1 of 1965 and the 350cc YR-1 of two years later. On the racetrack Yamaha's Phil Read won four 250cc titles, and other riders including Finnish ace Jarno Saarinen continued the firm's Grand Prix domination. In just a few years, Yamaha had risen from comparative obscurity to become one of the world's leading manufacturers. The YDS-2 had played an important part in that success.

Yamaha YDS-2 (1962)	
Engine	Air-cooled two-stroke parallel twin
Capacity	246cc (56 x 50mm)
Maximum power	25bhp @ 7500rpm
Transmission	Four-speed, chain final drive
Frame	Steel cradle
Suspension	Telescopic front, twin shocks rear
Weight	312lb (142kg)
Top speed	90mph (145km/h)

Below: The Yamaha's forks and shocks were criticised for being too soft in contemporary tests, but the Yamaha's twin leading-shoe front drum brake was praised.

BMW R69S

For refinement, effortless high-speed cruising ability and quality of construction, few bikes of the 1960s came close to matching BMW's R69S. But the 594cc boxer earned its reputation only after overcoming a shaky start, because, following its introduction in 1960, it suffered a series of engine failures that came as an unpleasant surprise to BMW, which had a long history of robust and reliable horizontally opposed twins.

The German marque's pushrod-operated boxer engine layout traced its ancestry to 1936, and the 494cc R5 model with which BMW had introduced overhead valves to its range, alongside the previous side-valve twins. Initially the R69S gave no sign of trouble, as it scored a series of track successes. In 1961, an S-model modified with taller gearing averaged 109mph (175km/h) to break the world 12-hour and 24-hour records. In the same year, the R69S was ridden to victory in both the Barcelona 24-hour race and the Thruxton 500-mile (805km) event for production machines.

The R69S was a sports machine, designed for hard and fast riding, and its 42bhp engine's problems were triggered by sustained high-speed riding, especially on German autobahns. Once the trouble was cured, with stronger crankcases and a vibration damper on the crankshaft, the boxer cruised with a pleasantly smooth feel at 80mph (129km/h), with performance in hand to a top speed of 110mph (177km/h). It was also stable and comfortable, although heavier than rival British twins. It remained in production until 1969, by which point more than 11,000 had been built.

Above: *By the time this R69S was built in 1964, BMW had modified its 594cc boxer engine with a crankshaft-mounted vibration damper that dramatically improved its reliability.*

Below: *The BMW's thick dual seat helped to make it comfortable, and the bike also handled well thanks partly to its firm and well-damped Earles forks.*

Royal Enfield Continental GT

T he racy red Continental GT, launched in late 1964, lasted barely a couple of years before being dropped from Royal Enfield's range. But the GT's short life was no reflection on its performance or impact. The 250cc single was a capable little machine, and was Royal Enfield's fastest-selling 250cc model of the 1960s.

The GT was the ultimate development of Enfield's 250cc pushrod single, which dated back to the original Crusader model of 1956. Several updates led to the 1963-model Continental, which was often modified by its owners with café-racing features including clip-ons, big glass-fibre petrol tanks and racing seats. Enfield boss Leo Davenport's brainwave was to incorporate many of those parts into a new model: the Continental GT.

The new sportster's main styling feature was its long red glass-fibre fuel tank. Other neat details included a flyscreen, clip-on handlebars, chromed headlamp, humped dual seat, and the front drum brake's dummy cooling rims of polished alloy. The engine's increased compression ratio and new exhaust pipe helped raise peak output to 21bhp.

Straight-line performance was lively for a small-bore single, with a top speed of 85mph (137km/h), and the engine's improved breathing system cured the previous oil leak problem. The remaining flaw was the five-speed gearbox, which was prone to false neutrals. Handling was excellent, aided by the GT's light weight and competent suspension. But the model's popularity could not prevent it from being dropped when, in 1967, struggling Royal Enfield's factory at Redditch in Birmingham was closed, and production of single-cylinder models ended.

Above: The Continental's light weight and taut suspension combined to give excellent handling, adding to the bike's sporty image.

Above left: Clip-on bars, flyscreen, glass-fibre tank, and the front brake's dummy cooling rims helped give the GT a racy look.

Royal Enfield Continental GT (1964)	
Engine	Air-cooled ohv 2-valve pushrod single
Capacity	248cc (70 x 64.5mm)
Maximum power	21bhp @ 7500rpm
Transmission	Four-speed, chain final drive
Frame	Steel single downtube
Suspension	Telescopic front; twin shocks rear
Brakes	Drum front & rear
Weight	300lb (135kg)
Top speed	85mph (137m/h)

Harley-Davidson Electra Glide

Above: The V-twin engine's new electric starter earned the Electra Glide its name. The 1208cc Panhead engine was used only in 1965 before being replaced by the Shovelhead.

Above left: This Electra Glide's accessory windscreen added to the comfort and practicality provided by the Harley's standard fitment footboards, buddy seat and panniers.

For two-wheeled touring in comfort and style, Harley-Davidson's Electra Glide has long held a unique appeal. Since its introduction in 1965 the Glide has become as much a part of American motoring legend as the Corvette and Mustang cars. It has undergone countless updates, starred in Hollywood movies (notably *Electra Glide in Blue*, in 1973) and fashioned a mighty reputation as a devourer of serious distances.

The original FLH Electra Glide was created when Harley added an electric starter to the 1208cc (74 cubic inch) V-twin engine of the Duo-Glide. The new model arrived at a critical time, with the US motorcycle market booming. Just a year later, the Milwaukee firm uprated its ageing Panhead powerplant with a redesigned, slightly more reliable and oil-tight pushrod V-twin unit whose aluminium cylinder heads earned it the nickname Shovelhead. The new motor also produced slightly more power, to a maximum of 54bhp at 5400rpm.

That extra engine performance was very useful, for the Electra Glide's pursuit of touring luxury had resulted in a large and heavy machine. When fully dressed with Harley's King of the Highway equipment – including windscreen, mudguard tips, Super Deluxe Buddy Seat, saddle-bags and Extra Quiet dual silencers – the bike weighed more than 365kg (803lb). But the Glide's elegance and comfort made it a success. And as Harley battled through the firm's 1969 takeover by American Machine and Foundry (AMF), the Electra Glide flagship went from strength to strength, playing a key role in the company's history.

Harley-Davidson Electra Glide (1965)	
Engine	Air-cooled ohv four-valve pushrod 45-degree V-twin
Capacity	1208cc (87 x 101mm)
Maximum power	60bhp @ 5400rpm
Transmission	Four-speed, chain final drive
Frame	Tubular steel
Suspension	Telescopic front; twin shocks rear
Brakes	Drum front & rear
Weight	783lb (355kg)
Top speed	100mph (161km/h)

Honda CB450

The CB450 was the bike with which the Japanese motorcycle industry stepped up to the big time. Until the 445cc twin was launched in 1965, the largest motorcycle engine that Honda had built was a 305cc twin based on a 250. Many people in the West were convinced that the Japanese would be content to stick to small-capacity bikes – until the CB450 shattered that illusion.

In many respects the CB450 was an enlarged version of smaller Honda twins such as the 250cc CB72, although its 43bhp engine featured a double overhead cam layout, plus unusual torsion bar valve springs. The bike's look also followed Honda's traditional style, with a humped and chrome-plated petrol tank plus a black paint finish that earned the bike the nickname 'Black Bomber'. Its chassis was based on a twin-cradle frame rather than the spine layout used by Honda's smaller machines and featured conventional telescopic forks and twin shocks.

With undramatic acceleration to a top speed of just over 100mph (161km/h), the CB450 was not fast enough to match British twins such as Triumph's Bonneville on pure performance. Instead it was marketed as a comfortable long-distance machine. It didn't sell particularly well in Britain, where there was some surprise that Honda didn't introduce a sportier version.

But the touring twin was more popular in the States, where its smoothness, generous midrange performance, comfort, sound handling and reliability were more highly valued. There was certainly no doubting its significance. The CB450's arrival confirmed that the Japanese had the whole of motorcycling in their sights.

Above: The CB450 was visually similar to Honda's smaller 250cc CB72, but its parallel-twin engine incorporated dohc valve layout.

Above: Although the CB450 was powered by Honda's biggest ever bike motor, it lacked the straight-line performance of 650cc British twins.

Dresda Triton

T he Triton was the supreme hybrid of 1960s British motorcycling: a blend of Triumph parallel-twin powerplant and Norton Featherbed-framed chassis that provided the speed and handling ability to outrun just about anything else on the road. Many firms and individuals assembled Tritons over the years, using a variety of motors and frames. Of them all, the best known were the machines that were built and successfully raced, both in Britain and abroad, by London dealer Dresda Autos.

Precise origins of the first Triton are unclear, because several similar machines were constructed independently in the 1950s. One was built by London-based racer/engineer Doug Clark, who fitted a Triumph 650cc engine into a Manx Norton frame in 1954. The bike was used both on road and track, as Clark rode it to the circuits where he was competing. Triumph was reportedly unhappy. The firm wrote to Clark threatening legal action if he continued with the project, and told its London dealers to refuse to sell him engine spares.

It was easy to understand the Triton's appeal in the early 1960s, when Norton and Triumph twins were among the fastest machines on the road. Triumph's 650cc Tiger 110 had held a straight-line advantage over its 600cc rival the Norton Dominator 99, and by the time Norton's more powerful 650SS arrived in 1962, Triumph's reputation for speed was secure. But Norton's Featherbed frame and Roadholder forks were superior to their Triumph equivalents, and also came with an impressive racing pedigree.

By providing the best of both worlds, the Triton became the ultimate high-performance parallel twin. Machines varied considerably, featuring different fuel tanks, instruments, seats, suspension parts, and exhaust systems. As well as Triumph's twin-carburettor 650cc Bonneville engine, Triton builders used 500cc

Above: *Key to the Triton is its combination of Triumph parallel-twin engine and Norton Featherbed frame. The large-radius rear curve shows this Featherbed is from a Manx single.*

Left: *This Triton's classical café-racer look is enhanced by clip-on bars, exposed fork springs, big twin leading-shoe front drum brake, humped seat and unfiltered Amal carbs.*

motors, and later the 750cc unit too. Norton's Featherbed frame came in original Wideline or later Slimline form, as well as being sourced from the Manx single.

One thing that almost all Tritons shared was the classical look, comprising long alloy fuel tank, clip-on handlebars, rearset footrests, and most of all the compact parallel-twin Triumph motor surrounded by the Featherbed frame's distinctively curved steel tubes. If the secret of the Triton's success was that it combined the best British engine and chassis, it's also true that much of its appeal came from its lean and uncluttered style.

The Triton's popularity leapt when firms including Dresda began producing conversion kits and complete machines. Dresda boss Dave Degens was a leading racer, and his victory (with co-rider Rex Butcher) on a Triton in the 24-hour race at Montjuic Park in Barcelona in 1965 boosted demand. Degens, who won at Barcelona again on a similar machine five years later, estimates that his firm built over 500 Tritons in the 1960s and early '70s, plus many Featherbed-style frames around which owners assembled Tritons of their own.

Even the Triton could not compete against more powerful Japanese and Italian machines in the 1970s. But its reputation as motorcycling's finest hybrid, and one of the great high-performance machines, is very much intact.

Dresda Triton (1965)	
Engine	Air-cooled ohv four-valve Triumph parallel twin
Capacity	649cc (71 x 82mm)
Maximum power	50bhp @ 6500rpm
Transmission	Four-speed, chain final drive
Frame	Steel twin cradle Norton Featherbed
Suspension	Telescopic front; twin shocks rear
Brakes	Drum front & rear
Weight	350lb (159kg)
Top speed	120mph (192km/h)

Opposite: *This 1965-model Triton, powered by a 650cc Bonneville engine, was one of many hundred built by London dealer Dresda, which continued production into the 21st century.*

Velocette Venom Thruxton

The fastest and most glamorous of Velocette's long line of 500cc singles was the Venom Thruxton. Introduced in 1965, it was essentially a tuned and race-kitted version of the Venom, Velocette's standard large-capacity model. Since the start of the decade, the Venom had been available in race-ready 'Clubman' spec, featuring clip-on bars and high-compression engine. In 1964 the Birmingham firm had also introduced a high-performance kit incorporating a new cylinder head plus large Amal Grand Prix carburettor.

A year later Velocette fitted the Venom Clubman with the performance kit to create the Thruxton, which also featured a big silver-painted petrol tank with a cut-out for the carb. Other features included a humped racing seat, rearset footrests, alloy wheel rims, and twin leading-shoe front drum brake with a scoop for cooling air. The Thruxton was expensive but it had the performance to match. The 41bhp engine gave a top speed of 105mph (169km/h), plus flexibility and 90mph (145km/h) cruising ability.

The Thruxton was not every rider's idea of a fast motorcycle. The single was often difficult to start, and was prone to loose bolts due to vibration. Its generally sound handling was compromised by occasional instability when ridden hard. But many Velocette enthusiasts were delighted by its unique blend of uncompromising character and race-derived performance, and the Thruxton sold well. Sadly for Velocette, even this ultimate single could not save the marque following its disastrous decision to produce scooters and the two-stroke LE commuter bike. Production finally ended in 1971.

Above: The Thruxton, with its racy lines and powerful 500cc engine, continued a line of sporty Velocette singles that stretched back to TT-winning machines of the 1920s.

Below: This Thruxton's notable features include its big twin leading-shoe drum, trademark Velo fishtail silencer, and the tank cut-out for the big Amal carburettor.

Suzuki T20 Super Six

The neat and lively T20 Super Six was the bike that brought Suzuki into the modern era. The little 247cc two-stroke twin's appeal was highlighted by an advertisement showing a leather boot flicking up the T20's gearlever, with the words: 'When the rest run out of power, shift into sixth!' Below the picture, Suzuki's distinctly optimistic claim of a 100mph (161km/h) top speed emphasised the bike's performance.

The Super Six, known as the X6 Hustler in the US, was based on Suzuki's T10, a modest roadster that had been introduced three years earlier and had become the firm's first model to be exported in serious numbers. Although its styling and engine layout were similar, the T20 was lighter and sportier, as well as having an extra gear. Larger carbs helped increased peak output to 29bhp; lubrication was by oil pump instead of pre-mix. A twin-downtube frame and tubular swing-arm replaced the T10's old-style pressed-steel chassis.

Suzuki's claims of 'ton-up' speed were exaggerated but the Super Six was good for 95mph (153km/h) – fast for a 250cc bike. It was also reliable, even when use was made of the 8000rpm redline. Handling was much improved from the T10, providing a firm ride with little of the instability to which rivals such as Yamaha's YDS-3 were prone. One 1966 magazine test described the Super Six as 'one of the most exciting bikes to appear in any capacity class for several years.' The little two-stroke certainly helped kick-start Suzuki's reputation for two-wheeled performance and led to a string of successful high-performance twins.

Above: The Super Six handled well but its main attraction was the outstanding straight-line performance provided by its rev-happy and reliable two-stroke parallel-twin engine.

Above: Suzuki uprated the 247cc powerplant with automatic lubrication plus the extra gearbox ratio that gave the Super Six its name.

Kawasaki 250SG

After a slow start, Kawasaki's motorcycle operation expanded rapidly in the late 1960s, with models including the single-cylinder 250SG. There was a simple explanation for the fast growth. The giant Japanese ship-, train- and plane-building corporation had taken over the long-established but struggling Meguro motorcycle firm in 1962. The SG had originally been sold in Japan as the Meguro S8.

The acquisition of Meguro gave Kawasaki a near-instant range from 650cc parallel twin to 50cc scooter – including the 248cc single that became the 250SG. Power and excitement were not part of the attraction. Its air-cooled motor used pushrod valve operation to produce 18bhp, and was held in a tubular-steel frame, with telescopic forks, twin rear shocks and drum brakes. Behind the sprung saddle was a luggage rack that could hold a pillion seat if required.

With either the Meguro or Kawasaki name on its tank, the single was a capable and well-engineered machine with a reasonable turn of speed. It cruised smoothly and reliably at 50mph (80km/h), with a top speed of about 70mph (113km/h). Its only real design flaw was the old-fashioned, four-speed gearbox's potentially disastrous ability to change directly from top into first.

The SG's handling and braking were also very adequate, and the single proved a useful asset for the recently formed Kawasaki Motorcycles. It remained in production for several years, helping the firm establish itself while leaving its engineers free to develop more glamorous bikes including the fearsome two-stroke triples and Z1 four.

Above: The SG's Meguro-developed, 248cc single-cylinder engine incorporated a four-speed gearbox whose design did not prevent the rider changing directly from top to first.

Left: The tank badge of this 1966-registered bike says Kawasaki, but the SG had been produced by Meguro when introduced on the Japanese market two years earlier.

Kawasaki 250SG (1966)
Engine Air-cooled ohv 2-valve pushrod single
Capacity 248cc (66 x 72.6mm)
Maximum power 18bhp @ 7000rpm
Transmission Four-speed, chain final drive
Frame Steel single downtube
Suspension Telescopic front; twin shocks rear
Brakes Drum front & rear
Weight 363lb (165kg)
Top speed 70mph (113km/h)

Bridgestone 350 GTR

Until the late 1960s Japanese industrial giant Bridgestone backed up its tyre manufacture by building a string of high-quality two-stroke motorcycles. The best of them was the 350 GTR, whose sophisticated 345cc parallel-twin engine differed from rival two-strokes by featuring rotary disc valve induction, which gave more precise control than the simpler piston ports normally used. This helped the GTR to an impressive peak power output of 37bhp, which it complemented with sound handling and high production quality.

The stylish and lightweight GTR was particularly notable for its acceleration, and could keep up with almost any other bike from a standing start. The Bridgestone was also stable at speed, with a notably refined feel. Its six-speed gearbox's tall top ratio kept maximum speed down to about 95mph (153km/h). But the motor's broad spread of torque, combined with the rubber-mounted powerplant's smoothness, meant that roadgoing speed was limited more frequently by the exposed riding position than by engine performance.

The GTR also handled very well, with the help of a rigid twin-cradle steel frame, plus firm and efficient suspension that typified Bridgestone's generally high-quality construction. Braking was impressive, too, due mainly to the reliable power of the twin leading-shoe front drum. If the GTR had a weakness it was price, because the refined twin was significantly more expensive than its Japanese two-stroke rivals. Relatively few were sold before Bridgestone abandoned motorcycle production in 1969 to concentrate on manufacturing the tyres for which the company is still well known.

Above: Raised handlebars and a tall top gear didn't help the GTR's high-speed performance, but the twin was still good for a respectable 95mph (153km/h).

Left: This immaculate GTR highlights the neat design and high build quality for which Bridgestone was known before the firm halted motorcycle production in 1969.

Bridgestone 350 GTR (1966)	
Engine	Air-cooled two-stroke parallel twin
Capacity	345cc (61 x 59mm)
Maximum power	37bhp @ 7500rpm
Transmission	Six-speed, chain final drive
Frame	Steel twin cradle
Suspension	Telescopic front; twin shocks rear
Brakes	Drum front & rear
Weight	330lb (150kg)
Top speed	95mph (153km/h)

Suzuki T500

In terms of performance for the money, few bikes came close to matching the T500 two-stroke twin with which Suzuki gained a foothold in the large-capacity motorcycle market of the late 1960s. The T500, known as the Cobra in the UK and the Titan in the United States, combined genuine 105mph (170km/h) performance with impressive reliability. Despite the fact that it undoubtedly lacked both glamour and sophistication, it had obvious appeal to many aspiring superbike riders on a tight budget.

In essence the T500, launched in 1967, was a larger version of the T20 Super Six two-stroke twin that had shaken up the 250cc market a year earlier. The heavily finned, 492cc air-cooled motor produced 44bhp and was flexible by two-stroke standards, giving thrilling acceleration with the help of the bike's relatively low weight of 411lb (187kg). The chassis was less impressive. Both frame and swing-arm were made from steel tubing of distinctly narrow diameter, and the forks and shocks were oversprung and underdamped.

Even so, the T500 generally handled acceptably, with the help of conservative steering geometry plus a friction steering damper. When ridden hard it could become very lively, and many owners replaced the original shocks with superior aftermarket units such as Girlings, which helped without completely curing the problem. Despite this, Suzuki did very little to update the T500 until 1976, when it was given a restyle, a disc front brake and a new name: GT500A. The twin stroker was still quick, cheap and crude; a classic poor boy's performance bike.

Above: Suzuki's torquey 492cc two-stroke engine was more than a match for the relatively thin steel frame that held it.

Below: The drum-braked GT was produced with few changes until 1976, when a restyle and disc brake created the GT500A.

BSA Spitfire MkIV

BSA's Spitfire was fast but flawed. Its 646cc engine was powerful, and for pure sprinting speed the Spitfire was arguably as good as BSA's parallel twins ever got. But throughout its life and despite two revamps, the Spitfire remained dogged by unreliability that ensured it never fulfilled its potential or sold as well as BSA had hoped.

The Spitfire replaced the Lightning Clubman as BSA's highest-performance machine in 1966. To the already high engine specification of the Lightning Clubman, the Spitfire – strangely the first model was called the MkII Special, although there had been no MkI – added Amal GP2 carburettors that raised peak power output to an impressive 54bhp.

Finished in red, the Spitfire came with a tiny fibreglass fuel tank and was very handsome. For a time it went as well as it looked, too. The hotted-up engine gave thrilling acceleration to a top speed of 120mph (193km/h), handling from the new chassis was more than acceptable, and overall performance matched that of any standard production machine. But sadly for Spitfire owners, that tuned engine was prone to major crankshaft problems.

The Spitfire MkIV of 1968 added Amal Concentric carbs and a big twin leading-shoe front drum brake to the specification, but BSA had done very little to make the engine more reliable. The twin was still fast, and handled and braked better than ever. If only its mechanical problems could have been cured, the Spitfire might not have been dropped from BSA's range just a year later, to make way for the Rocket III triple.

Above: The Spitfire MkIV added a big front drum brake and Amal Concentric carbs to the original Spitfire attractions of bright red paintwork and powerful parallel-twin engine.

Above: In Spitfire guise, BSA's 646cc motor produced an impressive 54bhp, but it remained prone to problems despite several years of development.

Norton Commando

Norton's Commando was one of the most famous and best loved of British bikes, its success stemming from the way that its innovative chassis used rubber mountings to reduce the vibration generated by its parallel-twin engine. That allowed the Commando's rider to make the most of the bike's engaging blend of torquey engine and capable handling, to which it added good looks and a generally high level of reliability.

The first Commando, launched in 1968, was a striking machine whose streamlined tailpiece earned the designation 'Fastback'. Its 745cc pushrod-operated power-plant was based on that of Norton's previous Atlas, with cylinders angled slightly forward instead of vertical. Other modifications including increased compression ratio boosted claimed maximum output to 58bhp, and the motor also featured a new single-plate diaphragm clutch.

The Commando's big advance was its new chassis, whose Isolastic system of rubber mounting was designed to tackle the vibration that had plagued larger-capacity parallel twins including the Atlas. The system was developed by a team headed by former Rolls-Royce engineer Dr Stefan Bauer. The frame comprised a large main spine plus twin downtubes. Rubber-mounted rear engine plates, isolated the motor while allowing the frame's spine to counter torsional stresses.

Provided its rubber bushes were well maintained, the Isolastic frame lived up to its name by significantly reducing vibration. It helped maintain Norton's traditionally high standard of handling, backed up by efficient Roadholder forks and Girling shocks. And the Commando also had the engine performance to match, with storming acceleration to a top speed of 115mph (184km/h). It was rapturously received, winning the prestigious Motor Cycle News Machine of the Year competition five years in a row.

The Commando was also a hit in the US, where it was sold with high, wide handlebars. Norton developed special versions for the US market, notably the 1971-model Commando SS, a street scrambler with a small fuel tank and high-level pipes, and the Hi-Rider with its chopper-style seat and high bars. For sportier riders there was the Combat Commando, which had flatter bars to complement its hotted-up 65bhp motor. But the Combat was an unreliable disaster because its engine could not handle the extra power.

Commandos were raced successfully in the early 1970s, despite generally being down on power compared to most rivals. Norton's works racer/engineer Peter Williams developed the Commando Formula 750, whose steel monocoque frame gave advantages in both weight and aerodynamics, and rode the innovative twin to victory against Japanese opposition in the 1973 Formula 750 TT.

Norton also continued to develop the roadgoing model, notably in 1973, when its engine was bored-out to create the Commando 850. This was produced in standard Roadster and larger-tanked Interstate options. The bigger motor's added torque gave a useful performance boost but the ageing parallel twin's limitations were highlighted by Norton's struggle to add a reliable electric starter. By the mid-1970s parent company Norton Villiers Triumph had slipped into financial problems. Production of the by then outdated Commando continued until 1977.

Above: This immaculate Commando features the long tailpiece that earned the first model the name 'Fastback', and has a disc front brake rather than the original drum.

Opposite: The rubber-mounted Commando engine's smoothness encouraged its rider to make the most of its performance – by keeping the needles of both speedometer and rev-counter spinning.

Norton Commando (1968)

Engine Air-cooled ohv four-valve pushrod parallel-twin

Capacity 745cc (73 x 89mm)

Maximum power 58bhp @ 6800rpm

Transmission Four-speed, chain final drive

Frame Steel spine with twin downtubes

Suspension Telescopic front; twin shock rear

Brakes Drum front and rear

Weight 420lb (190kg)

Top speed 115mph (184km/h)

Kawasaki W2TT Commander

The W2TT Commander did not live up to Kawasaki's optimistic advertising claim that it was 'The ultimate in motorcycles – speed, style, comfort, handling and safety for the sports rider', but it was an important model for the Japanese firm. It was with the dual-purpose parallel twin, launched alongside the similar W2SS roadster in 1967, when Kawasaki's motorcycle operation was still in its infancy, that the giant corporation moved with increasing conviction into the large-capacity motorcycle market.

Kawasaki had stepped up its bike operation in the early 1960s by taking over the ailing Meguro firm, whose copy of BSA's 500cc A7 parallel twin had been sold as the Meguro K1. In 1965 Kawasaki made a few modifications and released the twin as the K2. They then brought out an updated, 650cc version, the W1. Shortly after that came the tuned, twin-carburettor W2 models that would become Kawasaki's best-known early machines. The dual-purpose W2TT Commander's most notable difference from the W2SS roadster was its high-level, twin-pipe exhaust system on the left side.

The 624cc parallel-twin engine contained some significant differences from the BSA unit, and produced a respectable 53bhp. That was enough to give strong acceleration to a top speed of 110mph (177km/h), but vibration was severe at higher revs. Handling and braking were reasonable, and the Commander became popular in Japan, where the W2 was the best-selling big bike. The twin was less successful in export markets, but its arrival was further confirmation that Kawasaki had every intention of becoming a major motorcycling force.

Above: Kawasaki's 624cc parallel-twin engine was based on BSA's A10 unit, but incorporated numerous differences including the larger Y-shaped cover and separate four-speed gearbox.

Below: The W2TT Commander's high-level exhaust system distinguished the dual-purpose model from its roadster relations, the W2SS and the cheaper, single carburettor W1SS.

Triumph T150 Trident

The T150 Trident gave Triumph a fast and capable flagship, but the triple never quite lived up to its potential or became the success that the struggling company needed. Triumph had begun development of a three-cylinder roadster in 1965, but the project was delayed, largely due to opposition from the marque's American importer. Pressure from the US finally resulted in similar models being introduced in 1969 by Triumph and its sister firm BSA, whose Rocket Three housed the same 740cc powerplant in a modified chassis.

That delayed introduction was not the Trident's only problem, because its angular styling and aquamarine paint scheme proved unpopular. Its 58bhp engine featured traditional pushrod valve operation. The chassis was heavily based on that of Triumph's twins, including the frame, which was a strengthened version of their steel, single-downtube unit. Gaitered forks, borrowed from the twins, held stiffer springs to cope with the three-cylinder motor's extra weight.

Performance was excellent, especially when compared to the parallel twins that formed its main opposition. The Trident handled well, and its 125mph (200km/h) top speed and thrilling acceleration made it as quick as any rival in 1969. That included Honda's new CB750, but unfortunately for Triumph its triple couldn't match the sohc four's reliability or its specification, which included the disc brake and electric starter that the T150 lacked. If the Trident had been launched several years earlier it would surely have been a hit, but by the early 1970s it was not good enough to resist the Japanese superbike tide.

Above: *The first Trident's distinctive angular styling, aquamarine paint scheme and 'raygun' silencers were not well received, especially in the US.*

Above: *The T150 handled well thanks to a chassis that comprised a strengthened 650cc twin frame with uprated suspension.*

Moto Guzzi V7 Special

The V7 Special was an early star of Guzzi's V-twin line, which originated in curious fashion during the early 1960s with a tractor-like three-wheeled mountain vehicle called the 3x3. This was briefly produced for the Italian military before being abandoned, but Guzzi developed its 90-degree, pushrod-operated engine to power a motorcycle, the V7. In 1969 the Mandello firm enlarged the powerplant to 757cc and fitted it to a modified chassis to create the V7 Special.

The Special became popular due to its blend of simplicity, strength and relaxed cruising ability. Its softly tuned, 45bhp engine was a car-like device with dry clutch, four-speed gearbox and shaft final drive. The bike was designed for comfort more than speed, with high bars and a generous dual seat. Finished in white, it was often fitted with a tall screen and panniers. It accelerated crisply from low revs, cruised smoothly at 70mph (113km/h), had a top speed of 110mph (177km/h) and was very stable, thanks to a strong, steel-framed chassis and well-controlled suspension.

The V7 Special became highly regarded as a grand tourer well suited to covering large distances in style, with a distinctive long-legged feel. In 1971 it was modified to produce a special edition, initially for the US market, with higher bars and a rounded buddy seat: the California. For the following year Guzzi enlarged the engine to 844cc and fitted a five-speed gearbox. In just a few years, Italy's oldest motorcycle marque had established the V-twin dynasty that would lead it into the next century.

Moto Guzzi V7 Special (1969)	
Engine	Air-cooled ohv Four-valve pushrod 90-degree transverse V-twin
Capacity	757cc (83 x 70mm)
Maximum power	45bhp at 6000rpm
Transmission	Four-speed, shaft final drive
Frame	Steel twin cradle
Suspension	Telescopic front; twin shocks rear
Brakes	Drum front & rear
Weight	506lb (230kg) dry
Top speed	110mph (177km/h)

Below: This V7 Special is fitted with the windscreen and panniers that were popular accessories, enhancing the practicality provided by the Guzzi's smooth, shaft-drive V-twin engine and comfortable dual seat.

Above: Despite its size and weight the Guzzi was stable at speed and handled quite well, thanks to its strong frame, conservative geometry and capable suspension.

Yamaha XS-1

Yamaha made a belated but successful entry to the four-stroke market in 1969 with the XS-1, a parallel twin that was closely based on the dominant British twins of the day. The Yamaha's 654cc capacity, bore and stroke dimensions, and 360-degree crankshaft arrangement all followed those of BSA's Lightning. But the Japanese firm's 53bhp twin also incorporated differences including overhead camshaft instead of pushrod valve operation, and crankcases that were split horizontally instead of vertically in British style.

Designed mainly for the US market, the XS-1 looked lean and sporty despite high, wide bars. Its chassis was based on a twin-downtube steel frame, which held front forks whose rubber gaiters concealed external springs. Brakes were drums at both ends, with a powerful twin leading-shoe unit up front. Performance was lively, with strong midrange punch and a respectable top speed of 105mph (169km/h). The Yamaha suffered from typical parallel-twin vibration, but that was also true of its British rivals.

The XS-1's chassis was less competitive than its engine. The frame and swing-arm lacked rigidity, and the crude suspension also contributed to harsh ride over bumps, and some instability when ridden hard. Even so the twin was an enjoyable bike to ride. It sold well, especially in the US, before being uprated in subsequent years to create the slightly more refined and better handling XS-2 and XS650. The versatile parallel twins got Yamaha's four-stroke range off to a good start, and their successors remained popular throughout the 1970s.

Above: The Yamaha's slim and attractive styling was a vital part of its appeal, along with its impressively flexible and reliable 654cc parallel-twin engine.

Above: High, wide handlebars combined with high-rev vibration to limit the XS-1's high-speed capability, but helped make the twin pleasantly manoeuvrable at a more gentle pace.

Chapter 4

The 1970s

Honda CB750

The CB750's unprecedented combination of performance, sophistication and reliability made it a huge hit and launched the 1970s superbike era. Honda's powerful and smooth-running four had a massive influence on the bikes that followed. Such was its impact that it is widely accepted as the most important motorcycle ever built.

Sheer performance was a key aspect of the Honda's appeal. Vivid acceleration to a top speed of over 120mph (193km/h) put the four far ahead of most rivals on its launch in 1969. But more than pure speed, it was the Honda's level of refinement that made it special: its electric starter, disc front brake, five-speed gearbox, and most of all the four-cylinder powerplant and its eye-catching quartet of chromed exhaust pipes.

The 736cc, air-cooled engine's design was influenced by Honda's magical World Championship winning multi-cylinder racebikes of the 1960s, although the roadster's layout of single overhead camshaft and total of eight valves did not

Above: The CB750's unprecedented blend of overhead-cam four-cylinder powerplant and disc front brake caused a sensation when the bike was released. Honda's designers emphasised the engine layout by adding an attractive and free-breathing four-pipe exhaust system.

Left: Performance was stunning by early-'70s standards, and unlike most bikes the Honda was happy at high speed for as long as its rider could hold on.

Below: This CB750 was the first registered in Britain, in January 1970. The model was called the CB750 K0 in the US, where it was released in mid-1969.

match the exotic racers with their twin cams and four valves per cylinder. Peak output was an impressive 67bhp at 8000rpm, with strong low-rev performance plus a smoothness that most rival machines could not approach.

Equally importantly, the four-cylinder unit was notably robust and well engineered. By the time of the CB750's arrival, a generation of motorcyclists had grown up on smaller Hondas, and were confident that the Japanese firm's bikes would be reliable, and would have good electrics and no oil leaks. The CB750 exceeded expectations on all counts.

Chassis layout was based on a steel, twin-cradle frame that held the engine with cylinders angled slightly forward. The initial four was designed mainly as an all-rounder for the US market, and was a physically large bike with high bars and a wide seat. But, despite the exposed and upright riding position, it was well suited to cruising at speed.

When it was ridden hard, the Honda's combination of power, weight and flex-prone steel frame resulted in some instability. But most of the time it handled well enough, helped by firm suspension. Its powerful and fade-free single disc front brake gave an advantage in both image and performance over rival machines' drum brakes.

The Honda's competitive price also helped it to become an instant commercial success, especially in the US where most of the early production was sold. Honda even got a boost in 1970 when veteran racer Dick Mann won the Daytona 200 on a modified CB750. Sales took off in Europe, too, when the four arrived in early 1970. Rivals including Triumph's Trident and BSA's Rocket 3 triples seemed not merely outdated but the products of a previous generation.

Honda acted relatively slowly to update the original four, which was detuned slightly in subsequent years due to emissions regulations, and lost its performance lead when Kawasaki's 903cc, dohc Z1 arrived in 1973. But a variety of CB750 models remained popular, as did smaller variants including the CB500. The original four will long be remembered for transforming motorcycling and starting the superbike generation.

Honda CB750 (1969)	
Engine	Air-cooled sohc eight-valve four
Capacity	736cc (61 x 63mm)
Maximum power	67bhp @ 8000rpm
Transmission	Five-speed, chain final drive
Frame	Steel twin downtube
Suspension	Telescopic front; twin shocks rear
Brakes	Single disc front; drum rear
Weight	506lb (230kg) wet
Top speed	123mph (198km/h)

Yamaha YR-5

The 350cc YR-5 was among the first and best of Yamaha's string of fast and light two-stroke middleweights, which provided some of the outstanding bikes of the 1970s and '80s. Racetrack breeding was a vital part of the little twin's makeup. Yamaha's revvy, air-cooled two-stroke roadsters followed a string of impressive performances in the smaller Grand Prix classes during the 1960s, including world titles from British aces Phil Read and Bill Ivy.

The YR-5's design owed much to the YR1 of 1967, and was shaped both by racetrack development and by Yamaha's smaller roadsters. Slim and simply built, the YR-5 weighed just 330lb (150kg) with half a tank of fuel. It was the biggest of a visually near-identical family of 250, 200 and 125cc twins. Its piston-ported, 180-degree crankshaft motor produced a claimed maximum of 36bhp – which gave lively acceleration towards a top speed of just over 90mph (145km/h). The rev-happy YR-5 required regular gearchanging and plenty of revs to give of its best, but was capable of rapid and reasonably comfortable cruising until it came up against a hill or headwind.

Handling was light and agile, helped by a low centre of gravity and reasonably capable suspension. Wide handlebars and a narrow front tyre also helped the rider flick the bike into bends rapidly and effortlessly. The little twin was also well braked, reliable and competitively priced. Along with its similarly styled successor the RD350, which added a front disc brake and other improvements, it earned Yamaha an unmatched reputation for middleweight two-stroke performance.

Above: Yamaha's 347cc two-stroke twin engine was powerful and reliable, and would be uprated with extra performance and a six-speed gearbox in 1974 to create the RD350.

Below: The YR-5's slim styling was much more modern than that of Yamaha twins of a few years earlier, and helped make the twin a success in many countries.

Norton Commando 750S

T he 750S was arguably the most distinctive and stylish Commando variant that Norton produced during the early 1970s, following the original twin's introduction in 1968. It was aimed largely at the US market, especially California where desert racing was popular and Norton's Atlas twin had often been modified with a variety of off-road tweaks. High-level pipes, set-off by perforated heat shields, combined with the high handlebars, small fuel tank and rounded parallel-twin engine to make an eye-catching machine.

Norton fitted both the 750S and the Commando R roadster that was introduced at the same time with a Mk II version of the original 745cc pushrod engine. Revised ignition, increased compression ratio and free-breathing reverse-cone pipes helped increase peak output slightly, to 60bhp. The chassis retained the ingenious frame whose Isolastic rubber mounting system was a key part of the Commando's appeal. New, gaiterless front forks combined with several chromed details to enhance the S-model's flamboyant image.

Roadgoing performance was respectable, with strong midrange, a top speed of 115mph (185km/h), and smooth cruising thanks to the Isolastics. Despite its high bars the 750S was stable at speed, and its chassis maintained Norton's reputation for sound handling. Although Californian desert racers did not take to the 750S in large numbers, it was followed by a similarly styled model called the 750SS. With their high bars and tiny tanks, the dual-purpose twins were far from the most practical bikes Norton ever built. But for torque, handling and especially style, both models had plenty to offer.

Above: *Its shiny high-level exhaust system helped make the Commando 750S very stylish, but the Norton could not match the popularity of several rival dual-purpose twins.*

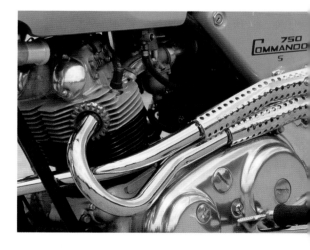

Above: *The 750S used Norton's MkII Commando motor, featuring higher compression ratio and increased maximum output of 60bhp.*

Harley-Davidson FX Super Glide

T he Super Glide was a vital part of Harley-Davidson's survival through difficult times in the early 1970s. Harley design director Willie G Davidson's striking V-twin, also known as the FX1200, is also regarded by many enthusiasts as the forerunner of the 'factory custom' – manufacturers' versions of the choppers and cruisers that were then being assembled by countless individuals. The Glide's format of large-capacity cruiser with a relatively sporty style pointed the Milwaukee firm in a new and important direction.

Essentially the Super Glide was a combination of the V-twin engine and rear end of Harley's giant Electra Glide and the front end of the (relatively) lightweight Sportster. Its powerplant was the 1200cc (74 cubic inch) Shovelhead unit, as fitted to the big tourer, with a Sportster-style two-into-one exhaust system. The electric starter was omitted, allowing fitment of a smaller battery on the right side. Styling included a broad fuel tank and the option of paintwork in patriotic red, white and blue, but was most notable for the 'boat-tail', a large glass-fibre seat/tail section.

The boat-tail proved unpopular and was promptly dropped for the 1972 sales season, but the Super Glide itself was a success. In subsequent years it became more performance oriented, being uprated with features including a slimmer tank, firmer suspension, disc brakes and an electric starter. The changes made the Glide more popular with each year, and it also formed the inspiration for other models, notably the Low Rider of 1977, that played a key part in Harley's revival.

Above: The Super Glide's patriotic red, white and blue paint scheme was well received but many dealers removed the 'boat-tail' rear section, which wasn't. In 1972 Harley replaced it with a standard rear mudguard, triggering the Glide's rise in popularity.

Harley-Davidson FX Super Glide (1971)

Engine Air-cooled ohv pushrod four-valve 45-degree V-twin

Capacity 1208cc (87 x 101mm)

Maximum power 65bhp @ 5500rpm

Transmission Four-speed, chain final drive

Frame Tubular steel

Suspension Telescopic front; twin shocks rear

Brakes Drum front & rear

Weight 560lb (254kg)

Top speed 110mph (177km/h)

BSA Lightning 650

BSA updated the Lightning – the high-performance version of its 654cc parallel twin – several times during the late 1960s and early '70s, most controversially in 1971. That was the year of the 'oil-in-frame' models, whose new chassis came with a taller seat that caused problems for shorter riders. Even before the Lightning entered production it was at the centre of a storm, because it was one of numerous 1971 models introduced by the struggling BSA/Triumph group at a lavish London dinner that became known as the 'last supper'.

In many respects the new Lightning was a sound bike. With its high bars, small tank and orange paintwork it was certainly stylish, if not particularly practical, with particular appeal for the US market. The Lightning had been the high-performance version of BSA's A65 unit-construction twin since 1965, featuring tuning parts including a higher compression ratio, hot camshafts, twin carburettors and a rev-counter. Its 52bhp powerplant was reasonably smooth and reliable, and gave strong acceleration to a top speed of about 110mph (177km/h).

The 1971-model Lightning's conical front drum brake was weak but the bike handled well, though that did not prevent BSA from redesigning its frame to lower the seat for the following year. The twin was also given a more traditional look including lower bars and a larger tank. But if BSA had got the Lightning right at last, they were too late. By this time the Birmingham firm was in serious financial trouble, and production of the twins ended shortly afterwards.

Above and below: This Lightning design lasted only one year before BSA revised the frame to lower the seat height. The 52bhp parallel twin engine was retained.

Laverda 750 SFC

The bright orange 750 SFC that Laverda launched in 1971 was not a race replica, it was the real thing: a genuine racing motorbike that just happened to be street-legal. The 744cc parallel twin was conceived by the small firm from Breganze in northern Italy as an endurance racing version of its 750 SF roadster, and was painted orange to make it more visible at night during 24-hour events. But the majority of SFCs were ridden on the street, after being fitted with a number plate and speedometer.

A clue to the SFC's intended role came with its initials, which stood for Sport, Freni (Italian for brakes, after its uprated drums) and Competizione, or competition. The racebike shared engine capacity and 360-degree crankshaft layout with the SF roadster, but most components were new, including the big Amal carburettors and high-compression pistons that helped increase peak output to 70bhp. The steel frame was modified to hold a fairing, and held upmarket suspension parts from Ceriani.

The result was a gloriously lean, single-minded machine that roared to 125mph (201km/h), and handled and stopped superbly. The SFC won its first race, the 1971 Barcelona 24 Hours. Fewer than 550 were built, many of which were converted to become some of the fastest and most charismatic bikes on the road. Appropriately enough, the SFC got even faster before production ended in 1976. Later models had electronic ignition and cast wheels plus the option of a hotter camshaft that increased top speed to over 130mph (217km/h).

Above: The SFC's half fairing encouraged its rider to make the most of the bike's considerable high-speed potential.

Below: Laverda's orange paintwork made the SFC stand out from the crowd, but it was the twin's uncompromising, race-bred layout and performance that earned it a cult following.

Kawasaki H2 750

awasaki's 748cc triple, known as the H2 or the Mach IV, was one of the most outrageous and aggressive bikes that a major manufacturer has ever produced. The air-cooled two-stroke was smoky, loud, thirsty and ill-handling. Most of all it was fast, earning a fearsome reputation for acceleration that was enhanced by distinctly dubious high-speed stability. On its arrival in 1972 it made a big impact on a motorcycling public eager for two-wheeled thrills.

The H2 was based on the similarly styled 500cc H1, also known as the Mach III, whose impressive performance had lifted Kawasaki's profile following its launch in 1969. The larger triple arrived three years later, with a 14bhp higher peak output of 74bhp, and a near-identical chassis based on a twin-downtube frame. The H2 also had considerably more midrange power, which combined with its relatively light weight of 454lb (206kg) to give scorching acceleration towards a top speed of 120mph (193km/h), often with its front wheel in the air.

Kawasaki's publicity material claimed that the H2 was 'so quick that it demands the razor-sharp reactions of an experienced rider', and few who rode it disagreed. That was particularly true because the Kawasaki's combination of power, light weight and relatively flimsy frame and suspension made it prone to wobbles, making the optional hydraulic steering damper advisable. Most owners were happy to put up with the handling, because the triple was competitively priced and reasonably reliable. And most of all, because it was so breathtakingly quick and exciting.

Above: High, wide handlebars were not ideally suited to a bike of the H2's fierce straight-line performance.

Below: The hydraulic damper below the steering head was a popular fitment to curb the H2's tendency to wobble at speed.

Suzuki GT750

The GT750 was not the most sleek and sophisticated machine in the years following its introduction in 1972. But the bulbous three-cylinder two-stroke was one of the most glamorous, and became one of the most popular early superbikes.

Suzuki's engineers created the GT around a 738cc, piston-ported two-stroke engine that was essentially one-and-a-half units from the air-cooled T500 twin. Retaining the twin's cylinder dimensions, and adding an extra cylinder plus liquid-cooling, boosted maximum output to 67bhp with a matching increase in midrange response. The chassis was conventional, with a twin-downtube frame, gaitered front forks and twin shocks.

The GT was a true Grand Tourer. Built as much for smoothness and comfort as for pure speed, it produced abundant midrange torque, had a roomy and comfortable riding position, and was a capable all-rounder that could cover large distances rapidly and with a certain style.

Above: The GT750's size, relaxed riding position and big dual seat marked it out as a bike built more for comfort than pure speed, and the two-stroke triple motor's broad power band added to its versatility.

Its look was unmistakable. The big Suzuki's rounded shape, unusual paint schemes and bulky liquid-cooled engine earned it the nicknames of 'Water Buffalo' in the US and the 'Kettle' in the UK. As well as the smooth, water-jacketed cylinders it stood out due to its large radiator and black-tipped reverse-cone silencers.

Straight-line performance was good rather than exceptional. The Suzuki's 524lb (238kg) of weight limited acceleration towards its 110mph (177km/h) top speed. The big triple was happiest being ridden relatively gently, when its rider could appreciate its long-legged feel and ability to cruise smoothly at around the legal limit.

Chassis performance also rewarded a relatively relaxed riding style. In most situations the GT was stable, if soft and ponderous, but more aggressive cornering resulted in the frame and suspension generating some unpleasant wallowing. Braking was reasonably good, thanks mainly to the twin-sided, twin leading-shoe front drum.

Hopes that Suzuki would develop a sportier triple came to nothing, although the firm did increase the power output slightly. The GT750L of 1974 produced 70bhp thanks to modifications including extra compression ratio, CV carbs and a new exhaust system. It was slightly faster but less smooth than the earlier model.

The liquid-cooled triple's tuning potential was shown by Suzuki's racing derivative, the TR750. It produced 100bhp and was the first bike to be timed at over 170mph (274km/h) at Daytona, but earned the nickname 'Flexy-flyer' with a vicious high-speed wobble. In its improved XR11 guise the TR was later raced to many wins by Barry Sheene and others.

Chassis updates to the GT750 roadster were limited to the introduction of a twin-disc front brake, plus details including a digital gear indicator and lockable fuel cap. They were not enough to keep the two-stroke in production after 1976, when motorcycle manufacturers came under pressure from tightening emissions laws and rising oil prices.

The GT750 is long gone, but it is not forgotten thanks to the enthusiasm of owners' organisations in many countries. Suzuki has built plenty of faster and more sophisticated machines over the years, but there is something special about the charismatic two-stroke triple.

Suzuki GT750J (1972)	
Engine	Liquid-cooled two-stroke triple
Capacity	738cc (70 x 64mm)
Maximum power	67bhp @ 6500rpm
Transmission	Five-speed, chain final drive
Frame	Steel twin downtube
Suspension	Telescopic front; twin shocks rear
Brakes	Drum front & rear
Weight	524lb (238kg)
Top speed	110mph (177km/h)

Above: The softly-tuned, liquid-cooled 738cc motor produced a modest 67bhp in standard form, but the 100bhp TR750 racing triple proved its tuning potential.

Left: The big Suzuki was ideally suited to effortless open-road cruising with plenty of acceleration in hand to its 110mph (177km/h) top speed.

BMW R75/5

The revised, so-called 'toaster tank' R75/5 that BMW launched in 1972, with its small, white-painted, chrome-sided petrol tank, was early evidence of the German firm's determination to appeal to more sporting riders than those who had previously been attracted by its conservative range of lookalike boxers with their big black tanks. On its launch three years earlier, the new-generation R75/5 had already broken the mould, being available in a choice of paint schemes, and abandoning the Earles fork front suspension system used in previous years.

Engine layout remained BMW's traditional air-cooled, two-valves-per-cylinder, pushrod-operated flat twin. But the 745cc unit's redesigned top section incorporated an electric starter and air filter housing, and other changes included alloy barrels and a strengthened shaft-drive transmission. The new frame had a single large-diameter top tube and twin downtubes, which curved upwards behind the engine, giving a look similar to that of Norton's Featherbed.

The R75/5 produced 50bhp and was respectably light at 418lb (190kg), which helped make it quick off the mark despite having only four gears. It cruised smoothly at 80mph (129km/h) and had a maximum speed of 110mph (176km/h). Front and rear drum brakes gave powerful stopping, and in bends the R75/5 lived up to the German marque's reputation for stable if less than sporty handling. More than its cornering speed, though, it was the BMW's blend of performance, practicality, build quality and long-distance comfort that endeared it to the minority of motorcyclists fortunate enough to be able to afford one.

Above: The chrome-sided 'toaster tank' gave the R75/5 a distinctive look, but proved unpopular with BMW customers and was soon dropped.

Below: Bing CV carbs helped the redesigned 745cc boxer motor produce 50bhp.

Moto Guzzi V7 Sport

Above: Guzzi's new engine kept the previous V7's transverse V-twin layout but had a reduced 748cc capacity. It was more powerful, lighter and more compact, and featured the alternator on the front of the crankshaft.

Above left: With its big front drum brake the Sport looked suitably racy, especially when its adjustable handlebars were in their lowest position. This 1973-model bike was one of the last produced.

Moto Guzzi's first true high-performance V-twin was the distinctive limegreen V7 Sport, which lived up to its name by being one of the world's fastest superbikes in the early 1970s, both in a straight line and around a racetrack. Guzzi had already established a solid reputation for touring oriented V-twins when, encouraged by breaking a string of world speed records at the Monza circuit in 1969, the firm from Mandello del Lario began development of a purpose-built sportster.

Capacity of the V7's engine was reduced from 757cc to 748cc, to allow entry in 750cc races. The 90-degree transverse V-twin was tuned with a new camshaft, increased compression ratio, lighter valve gear and unfiltered 30mm Dell'Orto carburettors to produce 70bhp at the crankshaft (52bhp at the rear wheel). A new alternator, bolted to the front end of the crankshaft, allowed engineer Lino Tonti to design a lower frame with a backbone in the previous generator's location between the cylinders. High-class cycle parts included Guzzi's own forks, plus Koni shocks and a big front drum brake.

The resultant V7 Sport was a stylish and wonderfully capable bike that combined fine handling with impressive straight-line speed. It was good for 125mph (201km/h), and cruised smoothly at the legal limit and beyond with an engagingly relaxed feel. Its high-speed stability was outstanding, and its cornering ability very good, with little adverse effect from the shaft final drive. Few rival superbikes could even approach its all-round performance, which confirmed Guzzi's arrival as a superbike force.

Moto Guzzi V7 Sport (1971)	
Engine	Air-cooled ohv four-valve pushrod 90-degree transverse V-twin
Capacity	748cc (82.5 x 70mm)
Maximum power	70bhp at 6300rpm
Transmission	Five-speed, shaft final drive
Frame	Steel spine
Suspension	Telescopic front; twin shocks rear
Brakes	Drum front & rear
Weight	495lb (225kg) wet
Top speed	125mph (201km/h)

Triumph X-75 Hurricane

With its trio of exhaust pipes plus a uniquely curvaceous tank-seat unit that highlighted its 740cc three-cylinder motor, Triumph's X-75 Hurricane was one of the most stylish bikes of the early 1970s – and one of the hardest accelerating. The Hurricane concept originated with Triumph's importer in the US, where the T150 Trident's angular styling was unpopular. The new triple was shaped in the States, without Triumph's knowledge, by young freelance designer Craig Vetter, later famous for making fairings and luggage.

Vetter replaced the original bodywork with a slender fibreglass form that blended the fuel tank into the sidepanel area. The tiny gas tank was impractical, but the visual effect was stunning. The 60bhp engine's cylinder head fins were enlarged to add visual impact, and gearing was lowered. Handlebars were raised, front forks were lengthened, and many other parts were modified. Exhaust downpipes slanted across the front of the motor, then ran back to the bank of upswept silencers on the right.

Acceleration in the lower gears was terrific, thanks to the Hurricane's relatively light weight and short gearing. Its 115mph (185km/h) top speed was 10mph (16km/h) down on that of the Trident, but standing quarter-mile time was half a second quicker. High-speed handling was dubious due to the bike's combination of high bars and kicked-out forks. But the X-75 was less about performance than style and attitude. The Trident was a better all-round bike but the Hurricane's looks and acceleration earned it a cult following, especially in the US.

Above: The Hurricane's unique exhaust system emphasised the bike's three-cylinder engine layout.

Below: Vetter's flowing tank-seat unit gave the triple an unmistakable look, enhanced by lengthened forks and the trio of exhaust pipes.

Ducati 350 Scrambler

With its high handlebars, punchy single-cylinder engine, agile chassis and rugged styling, Ducati's Scrambler combined lively roadgoing performance with genuine off-road ability. Ducati produced three visually similar Scrambler models during the early 1970s, with engines of 250, 350 and 450cc. The largest model's desmo valve gear gave little advantage, and many Ducati enthusiasts regarded the simpler 350cc model as the pick of the trio.

The Scrambler originated in the early 1960s, with off-road competition bikes that Ducati built for events such as the International Six Day Trial. Later the Italian marque introduced less exotic dual-purpose versions. The Scrambler was updated throughout the 1960s, keeping its unsilenced exhaust system but gradually losing its competition image as it gained improved lights, a battery, and roadster-type tyres in place of the original knobblies. By the early 1970s Ducati had introduced the street-legal singles, featuring yellow or orange tanks with chromed sides, for which the Scrambler name became best known.

The 350 had a capacity of 340cc and featured a high-compression piston, hot camshaft (driven by bevel gear), and short roadster silencer. Peak output was 25bhp. Given the bike's weight of just 293lb (133kg), that was enough to provide strong acceleration to a top speed of about 90mph (145km/h), although single-cylinder vibration intruded before that. A rigid frame and high-quality suspension gave agile handling with stability. The Scrambler's blend of style and all-round performance made it popular in many countries including Italy and the US before production ended in the mid-'70s.

Above: The Scrambler's slim lines and chrome-sided fuel tank helped make the single an attractive machine, and its versatile performance added to the appeal.

Above left: The midranking 340cc engine used bevel drive to its single overhead camshaft, but did not have the desmo valve gear of the larger 450cc unit.

Kawasaki Z1

Kawasaki's Z1 four took superbike performance to a different level when it howled onto the scene in 1973. Its 903cc engine was not only considerably larger than the 736cc unit of the Honda CB750 that had revolutionised motorcycling four years earlier, it also boasted twin overhead camshafts that helped give a maximum output of 82bhp – fully 15bhp up on the sohc Honda's figure. The result was a stunningly rapid bike that was in a class of its own for speed and adrenaline production.

Ironically it was the CB750 that led directly to the Z1's engine capacity and resultant power output, because in 1968 Kawasaki's engineers had been well on the way to completing a 750cc four project – nicknamed New York Steak – before being shocked by the CB750's unveiling. The Honda's subsequent success gave Kawasaki all the incentive needed to create a significantly more powerful and faster machine.

Below: As if the Z1's fearsome performance was not enough of an attraction, the Kawasaki was also very stylish, highlighted by its muscular dohc engine and the neat duck-tail rear end.

Kawasaki Z1 (1973)
Engine Air-cooled dohc eight-valve four
Capacity 903cc (66 x 66mm)
Maximum power 82bhp @ 8500rpm
Transmission Five-speed, chain final drive
Frame Steel twin downtube
Suspension Telescopic front; twin shocks rear
Brakes Single disc front; drum rear
Weight 542lb (246kg) wet
Top speed 132mph (212km/h)

Left: This bike is a 1974-model Z1-A, differing from the previous year's original model in its paint scheme and alloy (instead of black) cylinder finish.

Having created a bike of outstanding performance, Kawasaki gave it looks to match. The Z1's curved petrol tank, small sidepanels and rear duck tail combined with the big, heavily finned air-cooled powerplant to make a very handsome machine. Chassis specification was conventional. The engine was angled slightly forward in a twin-downtube steel frame whose forks held a 19-inch wheel and single brake disc. High, wide handlebars resulted in a wind-blown riding position but helped the rider manoeuvre the physically big four, which weighed a substantial 542lb (246kg).

Brutal acceleration was the Z1's most thrilling attribute. The big twin-cam motor delivered huge reserves of torque from low revs, sending the bike storming to a top speed of over 130mph (209km/h) at a rate that riders of other bikes could only dream about. It was also impressively smooth, even when running up to its 9000rpm redline. Equally importantly the big motor proved superbly reliable, even when fitted with the tuning parts soon developed by a host of eager specialists.

The Z1's chassis also benefited from attention, because the bike's blend of power, weight and relatively simple frame and suspension caused a few problems. For restrained riding the Kawasaki was well controlled and reasonably comfortable, despite its high bars. But its high-speed stability was marginal, especially under aggressive cornering. Many riders fitted a hydraulic steering damper, which helped. Others turned to custom-made chassis from specialists including Harris, Bakker, Moto Martin, Egli and Bimota.

Plenty of other owners were more than happy with the standard Z1, whose fearsome reputation added to its appeal. Such was the Z1's lead over the opposition that Kawasaki barely had to update it for several years. Eventually in 1976 a second front brake disc, previously an optional extra, was fitted as standard, and the bike was renamed the Z900.

At the same time the engine was detuned slightly, with new carbs and pipes, to reduce emissions for the US market. By then the big four was firmly established as the King of the Road, and had earned Kawasaki an enviable and lasting reputation for brutal, unburstable four-cylinder performance.

Below: When pushed hard in corners the Z1's power and weight were too much for its chassis, making fitment of a steering damper advisable.

MV Agusta 750 Sport

MV Agusta's multi-cylinder racebikes dominated the 500cc World Championship during the 1960s, but it was only with the arrival of the 750 Sport in 1973 that the Italian marque brought that glamour and performance to the street. MV boss Count Domenico Agusta had been reluctant to dilute his team's achievements with a roadgoing four, and had eventually released a 600cc tourer with curious styling, shaft final drive and modest performance. It had been an expensive failure.

The 750 Sport was totally different – an aggressive superbike with bright paintwork, clip-on bars and a humped racing seat. Its 743cc engine was based on that of the tourer, with gear drive to twin overhead cams. Unfiltered Dell'Orto carburettors, high-compression pistons and a quartet of shiny megaphone pipes helped lift peak output to 65bhp. Even the Sport had shaft final drive, and a frame that derived from the tourer rather than MV's racers. But it benefited from exotic cycle parts including Ceriani suspension, alloy wheel rims and Grimeca brakes; initially a big drum and later twin discs.

Straight-line performance didn't match factory claims, the true top speed being a rather disappointing 115mph (185km/h). Handling was also compromised by the bike's shaft drive and 506lb (230kg) of weight. But the Sport delivered strong and smooth acceleration, with a glorious howl from its exhaust, plus handling and braking performance that exceeded those of most superbikes. The hand-built MV was hugely expensive, but for the small number of riders who could afford one it was an utterly exhilarating machine.

Above: Fitting MV's optional full fairing hid the gorgeous dohc four-cylinder engine but enhanced the Sport's authentic race-replica look.

Above: The Sport was magnificently fast and loud but didn't match MV's performance claims.

BMW R90S

B
MW's refined R90S was arguably the finest all-round superbike of the mid-1970s. Resplendent in its distinctive smoked grey or orange paint scheme, the R90S was the sporting flagship of a line of flat-twins that stretched back half a century to BMW's first motorcycle in 1923. Some superbike rivals were more powerful; others more agile. But none could match the refined German boxer's combination of relaxed high-speed cruising ability, fine handling, reliability and impeccable finish.

Its 898cc powerplant was a tuned version of BMW's air-cooled R90/6 unit, complete with traditional pushrod valve operation and shaft final drive. Larger Dell'Orto carburettors and increased compression ratio helped increase maximum output to 67bhp. The R90S's top speed of around 125mph (200km/h) was impressive, as were its strong and responsive midrange acceleration and its smoothness throughout the range. Equally importantly, the bike's blend of flat handlebars and stylish bikini fairing allowed relaxed high-speed cruising.

Handling was good by contemporary standards, aided by the twin's relatively light weight of 474lb (215kg) with fuel. The fairly soft suspension worked well, and the brakes, which were uprated for 1975 after initial complaints, were subsequently adequate. Useful features included a dashboard clock, plus generous fuel range and a seat that allowed the rider to make the most of it. BMW's flagship had a price that matched its high specification: in many markets it cost more than twice as much as Honda's CB750 four. But for covering long distances at speed, few superbikes came even close to matching it.

Above and below: The R90S's combination of bikini fairing and smoked paintwork gave an unmistakable look that perfectly reflected the BMW flagship's unmatched combination of build quality and all-round performance.

Benelli 750 Sei

Benelli's 750 Sei became the world's first six-cylinder superbike on its launch in 1974, and came backed by the Italian marque's four-stroke racing pedigree, which included victory in the 250cc world championship in 1969. The Sei combined its unique engine layout with high-quality chassis parts. But despite its glamorous specification, the conservatively styled Sei contained little advanced engineering. Its 748cc, sohc engine, commonly criticised as resembling one-and-a-half Honda CB500-four units, produced a modest 71bhp, which meant the Benelli lacked the performance of the best rival Italian superbikes.

The six-cylinder engine was commendably narrow. A trio of dual-manifold Dell'Orto carbs left the rider plenty of kneeroom, as well as providing crisp throttle response and plenty of midrange torque. But although the softly-tuned Sei cruised with impressive smoothness, its large frontal area contributed to relatively tame acceleration and a top speed of only 115mph (185km/h). Chassis performance was more impressive, for despite its big motor the Benelli handled well. Its strong steel frame held high-quality Marzocchi suspension. Twin Brembo front discs gave powerful braking.

Benelli had hoped that the Sei's unique engine layout would add sufficient glamour to make the bike popular. But its unexceptional performance and high price proved more relevant than its number of cylinders and the fact that it was a capable all-rounder. Despite slow sales, the Sei remained in production throughout the 1970s with few changes, before its engine was enlarged to create the more powerful – but no more successful – 900 Sei.

Benelli 750 Sei (1974)	
Engine	Air-cooled, sohc 12-valve transverse six
Capacity	748cc (56 x 50.6mm)
Maximum power	71bhp @ 8500rpm
Transmission	Five-speed, chain final drive
Frame	Steel twin cradle
Suspension	Telescopic front; twin shocks rear
Brakes	Twin discs front; drum rear
Weight	484lb (220kg)
Top speed	115mph (185km/h)

Below: The Sei had restrained styling but there was no mistaking its unique engine layout, which was enhanced by the six-pipe exhaust system. This bike is fitted with Benelli's accessory rear carrier.

Above: The Benelli did not have outstanding straight-line performance but its flexible and smooth 748cc six-cylinder motor gave effortless cruising potential.

Triumph T160 Trident

The T160 Trident was launched in 1975 as a much needed follow-up to financially troubled Triumph's original 750cc triple, the T150 Trident, which had received a mixed reception following its introduction six years earlier. The new Trident's most important feature was arguably its comprehensively updated look. The old triple's angular fuel tank was replaced by a wider, more rounded tank whose shape and two-tone paintwork made the T160 a much more handsome machine.

The air-cooled, 740cc pushrod engine was basically that of the T150, incorporating modifications including an electric starter and left-foot gear change. Peak output was an unchanged 58bhp at 7250rpm. The engine was angled forward in a new steel frame, the layout of which owed much to Triumph's works production racers including Slippery Sam, the legendary Production TT winner. The twin lower frame tubes were raised for improved ground clearance, the engine sat higher and further forward, steering geometry was steepened, and the swing-arm was lengthened.

Performance was excellent and the Trident was an exhilarating bike to ride, with storming acceleration, a pleasantly rev-happy feel and a top speed of 125mph (200km/h). Although the triple was heavy, it handled well, thanks partly to excellent suspension that allowed the Triumph to sweep through curves that would have put many rivals into a wobble. That was not enough to make the triple a success, partly due to Triumph's mounting financial problems, which resulted in some unreliability. By the end of 1975, Norton Villiers Triumph was in receivership and Trident production had ended.

Above: Triumph gave the T150's 740cc pushrod motor an electric starter and left-foot gear change, and tilted it forward to fit in the T160's new, race-developed frame.

Below: The Trident's revised styling and impressive performance had plenty of appeal, but the bike arrived too late to save Triumph.

Suzuki RE-5

Suzuki's large, curiously styled and lavishly equipped RE-5 seemed like a machine from a different planet on its launch in 1975. The liquid-cooled, rotary-engined machine incorporated a breathtaking level of innovative and complex engineering. European manufacturers DKW and Norton already had Wankel rotary-engined models, but no previous bike approached the specification of the RE-5 with its two cooling systems, a two-stage carburettor, two lubrication systems and even two ignition systems.

The rotary powerplant produced 62bhp, which was good for a motor with an official capacity of 497cc but less than the output of Suzuki's simpler and cheaper GT750 triple. Performance was very respectable by mid-1970s standards. Contemporary tests recorded the top speed at about 110mph (177km/h), slightly down on the GT750's. The RE-5 was also just as good at high-speed cruising, thanks partly its engine's smoothness. The big, heavy Suzuki handled rather ponderously, though it made a comfortable tourer provided its rider could put up with another rotary trait, its heavy fuel consumption.

The RE-5's overall performance, allied to its distinctive style and engine design, caused much excitement when the bike was launched. But a price comparable to that of Kawasaki's Z1 four ensured that sales were very poor, worsened by a technical problem that delayed US introduction by several months. A 1976 restyle did little to help. By the end of that year Suzuki had abandoned production, despite the huge amounts of time and money invested in the project.

Above: Suzuki's rotary engine was powerful and smooth, but its complexity and poor fuel economy combined with teething problems to condemn the RE-5 to failure.

Below: The original RE-5 was visually striking as well as technically advanced. It featured an innovative cylindrical instrument panel whose plastic cover flicked back automatically when the ignition key was turned.

Ducati 900SS

Above: *Few rival superbikes could even approach the speed or riding sensation of a 900SS in full flight, with its long-legged feel and thunderous V-twin exhaust note.*

D ucati's lean, loud 900SS was proof of the beauty that could result from a motorcycle designed purely for speed. Single-minded to the point of being starkly functional, the booming Super Sport V-twin blended track heritage with a complete absence of frills. It was launched in 1975 as a development of the 750SS, a limited-edition replica produced to celebrate Paul Smart's victory in the prestigious 1972 Imola 200 race. The 750SS was so successful that the factory built more, then enlarged the engine to 864cc to create the 900SS.

Its 90-degree V-twin used bevel-gear drive to single overhead cams, plus desmodromic valve operation. Sucking in through huge, unfiltered 40mm Dell'Orto carbs and exhaling freely through Conti pipes, the 900 produced a healthy 79bhp. Notably slim and uncluttered, lacking even indicators or an electric starter, the 900SS scaled just 414lb (188kg). With its rider gripping clip-ons behind the silver and blue half fairing, the Ducati roared to over 130mph (209km/h) and cruised at high speed with an intoxicatingly smooth long-legged feel.

Equally importantly, the ultra-stable handling provided by its rigid steel frame and stiff Marzocchi suspension meant that the 900 could be held flat out through bends that forced rivals to shut-off. And when the rider did need to slow, there were no better brakes in motorcycling than the Ducati's trio of Brembo discs. The 900SS remained in production for almost a decade, although some later models were detuned. Mike Hailwood's famous 1978 TT victory inspired the following year's successful Mike Hailwood Replica version of the V-twin, featuring a full fairing in Hailwood's green and red paint scheme.

Above: *The Ducati's uniquely uncompromising specification included big twin front discs, a half fairing and single seat, but not such luxuries as indicators or an electric starter.*

Honda GL1000 Gold Wing

Purpose-built touring bikes have evolved so much since the Honda Gold Wing's launch in 1975 that the original GL1000 seems almost inadequate for serious long-distance riding. Yet when the GL was introduced, its size, style and sophistication polarised opinions between riders in the US, where the flat-four engined Honda's smoothness and comfort were immediately recognised, and European markets where the bike's size and complexity led to heavy criticism.

The fuss in the UK bike press, in particular, seems curious in retrospect because the subject of the debate was a bike whose unfaired layout and softly-tuned 999cc engine gave little hint of the huge, fully faired and lavishly equipped machine that the Gold Wing was later to become. The GL1000 had no fairing, top-box, passenger back-rest or panniers. No sound system or cruise control, and certainly no reverse gear, as on more recent Wings.

Honda's development team had begun work in 1972. Their first prototype was a 1470cc flat six, code-named the AOK. But although the engine reportedly worked well, its length created problems. Instead, Honda's engineers opted for a flat-four engine featuring single overhead camshafts driven by toothed belts. Peak power output was 80bhp.

The Wing's chassis was relatively conventional, based around a tubular-steel frame, though it incorporated a dummy fuel tank that contained a kick-start lever and a small amount of storage space. Fuel lived under the seat, which helped lower the centre of gravity of a bike which, at 638lb (290kg) with fuel, was far heavier than contemporary superbikes.

Straight-line performance was impressive; not so much the 120mph (193km/h) top speed as the long-legged cruising ability provided by the smooth-running flat-four motor. Despite its weight, the Wing accelerated at a thrilling rate, too. Its

Above: The original Wing's 999cc engine sat under a dummy tank, and was fed with fuel from a tank beneath the seat. The flat-four unit was smooth, flexible and had a low centre of gravity.

Left: For such a big, heavy bike the Gold Wing handled well but it was best suited to touring on long, relatively straight roads in the US.

Above: The original GL1000's simple, unfaired layout gave no hint of the luxurious, comprehensively equipped tourer that the Gold Wing would become in future years.

time of just under 13 seconds for the standing quarter mile put it behind only Kawasaki's Z1 in the superbike charts.

The GL1000 incorporated some notable flaws, most obviously its small under-seat fuel tank, which gave a range of less than 100 miles (161km) at speed; and the fact that the exposed riding position and hard seat made even this modest distance uncomfortable. Other problems included the uselessly pessimistic fuel gauge, which was set into the dummy tank and got in the way of a tank bag.

For such a heavy machine the Honda handled improbably well. Although it always felt like a big bike, its suspension was reasonably well controlled and the flat-four engine's low centre of gravity aided slow-speed manoeuvres. The wide bars made steering fairly light, despite the long wheelbase and 19-inch front wheel.

The GL1000's unsuitability for spirited riding was one reason for its mixed reception in Europe. But that mattered little to the older, touring-oriented US riders who rapidly adopted the smooth, quiet and refined Honda with great enthusiasm, often adding accessories ranging from fairings and luggage to extra chrome and lights. The cult of the Gold Wing had arrived, and motorcycle touring would never be quite the same – especially after 1980, when Honda added a fairing and hard luggage to the standard package.

Honda GL1000 Gold Wing (1975)	
Engine	Liquid-cooled sohc eight-valve flat four
Capacity	999cc (72 x 61.4mm)
Maximum power	80bhp @ 7500rpm
Transmission	Five-speed, shaft final drive
Frame	Steel twin downtube
Suspension	Telescopic front; twin shocks rear
Brakes	Twin discs front; disc rear
Weight	638lb (290kg) wet
Top speed	122mph (196km/h)

Honda CB400F

T he CB400F was a genuine mini-superbike, complete with unburstable four-cylinder engine, 100mph (161km/h) performance, sound handling, and neat styling incorporating the novelty of a four-into-one exhaust system. The little four was a landmark for Honda because it was the firm's first bike built specifically for the European market, with sporty features including flat bars, slightly rearset footrests, firm suspension and a 10,000rpm redline.

This was not the first smaller four that Honda had launched in the wake of the CB750. The CB500F of 1971 had been followed by the CB350 four, which Soichiro Honda said was the finest, smoothest bike his firm had produced – but which was expensive and rarely seen in Europe. In 1975 Honda increased the sohc engine's capacity to 408cc to power the restyled and less expensive CB400F. Its blend of style, 80mph (129km/h) cruising ability, excellent all-round performance and competitive price made it very popular in Europe, although predictably it sold less well in the US.

The four's success resulted in it remaining almost unchanged for several years. The later CB400F2 differed only in its paintwork plus a few details including pillion footrests mounted on solid subframe loops, rather than the swing-arm. Ironically it was competition from Honda itself that did most to put the 400F out of production. The twin-cylinder CB400T, launched in 1977, lacked the four's style and character but was slightly faster, handled just as well and was cheaper. The CB400F's reign as king of the four-stroke middleweights was over.

Above: The 400-four's sporty character was enhanced by the excellent handling provided by its blend of strong steel frame and relatively firm, well-damped suspension.

Below: This Honda's paint scheme and slightly raised handlebars indicate that it's a US-market CB400F2. The original four came in a choice of bright red or dark blue, and European versions had flatter bars.

Bultaco Metralla 250 GTS

T he 250 GTS was the last and most sophisticated of the rapid Metralla two-stroke singles that Spanish marque Bultaco built during the 1960s and '70s. The Barcelona firm introduced the first Metralla in 1962, powered by a 196cc single engine, and four years later increased capacity to 244cc to power the Metralla Mk2. Bultaco hit the headlines in 1967 when tuned Mk2s averaged over 88mph (142km/h) to take first and second places in the Isle of Man Production TT.

Bultaco struggled in the early '70s, but hit back in 1976 with a new-generation Metralla, the GT. To the earlier format of 27bhp two-stroke single engine the GT added fresh styling and higher bars, plus the sophistication of electronic ignition and indicators. Two years later it was followed by the Metralla GTS, which introduced a six-speed gearbox – and which retained the raw, race-bred character that had made the earlier Metrallas so popular. It was loud, light, supremely agile, and screamed to an indicated 100mph (161km/h).

That performance was respectable from a 250cc bike in 1978, although twin-cylinder Japanese rivals meant the GTS was less competitive than its Mk.2 namesake. Bultaco's bigger problem was the series of strikes that crippled production, resulting in the factory closing temporarily in 1979. Instead of being the bike from which Bultaco developed new models for the '80s, the Metralla GTS was left as a reminder of the days when Spanish singles were among the fastest and most exciting little bikes on the roads.

Above: *The Bultaco's single-cylinder engine differentiated it from many of its fastest 250cc twin-cylinder Japanese rivals.*

Below: *This GTS is an early model, as later versions featured cast wheels plus front and rear disc brakes.*

Yamaha XT500

Yamaha's XT500 was one of the unlikeliest two-wheeled hits of the 1970s. The big four-stroke single not only triggered renewed interest in dual-purpose bikes but also showed that a Japanese manufacturer could create an outstanding version of the traditional British 'thumper'. The XT was designed specifically for the US market, where tightening emissions legislation was causing problems for dual-purpose Japanese two-strokes. The US riders' enthusiastic response persuaded Yamaha to make the XT available in other countries too.

The XT's key attribute was inevitably its air-cooled, 499cc sohc engine, which had slightly oversquare bore and stroke dimensions but managed to deliver the flexible character of a traditional long-stroke single. Its 32bhp peak output gave a top speed of about 90mph (145km/h), and more importantly the XT was reasonably smooth and delivered crisp torque from low revs. It was also neatly and simply styled, and handled well thanks partly to a dry weight figure of just 328lb (149kg).

Yamaha acted quickly to improve the XT, adding details including a stronger engine bash-plate, more tucked-in exhaust and rubber-mounted indicators to the 1977 version that became the most popular in the model's long history. Further modifications including an alloy fuel tank and uprated suspension took the XT into the 1980s, and it was later further developed to create the XT600 plus upmarket Ténéré versions. These were inspired by the Yamaha's outstanding performance in desert races, notably the Dakar Rally – the first two editions of which were won by French XT500 rider Cyril Neveu.

Above: The XT500's clean styling and versatile performance quickly made it popular in the US, and led to the single becoming a success in other countries, especially when it was made more robust by modifications including a stronger bash-plate and revised exhaust.

Yamaha XT500 (1976)

Engine	Air-cooled sohc 2-valve single
Capacity	499cc (87 x 84mm)
Maximum power	32bhp @ 6500rpm
Transmission	Five-speed, chain final drive
Frame	Steel single downtube
Suspension	Telescopic front; twin shocks rear
Brakes	Drum front & rear
Weight	328lb (149kg)
Top speed	90mph (145km/h)

Suzuki GT550

Suzuki's air-cooled GT triple provided many riders with plenty of performance and value for money in the mid-1970s, without ever quite capturing the imagination in the fashion of its sportier two-stroke rivals from Kawasaki and Yamaha. The 550's lively acceleration and 100mph-plus (160km/h-plus) top speed meant that it was outclassed only by the fastest of superbikes. But its image was more that of an all-rounder, in the style of Suzuki's bigger triple, the liquid-cooled GT750 flagship.

The GT550, known as the Indy in the US, featured Suzuki's Ram Air System – in reality a simple piece of bent metal that helped direct cooling air over the cylinder head. The piston-ported two-stroke triple engine produced a maximum of 53bhp, and was held by a typical twin-cradle steel frame. Rounded styling, a generous dual seat and a weight figure of 451lb (205kg) confirmed that the GT was designed for comfort and practicality as much as speed.

Its performance was respectable, even so, with a top speed of close to 110mph (175km/h) and spirited acceleration provided the revs were kept near the 7500rpm redline. Handling was mixed, with the triple's agility at lower speeds marred by firm suspension and a tendency to wobble when ridden hard. Those chassis limitations and the two-stroke's thirst limited the GT's appeal, as did the attraction of four-stroke middleweights – including, after 1977, Suzuki's own GS550 four. The GS was more expensive and no faster, but its superior handling and fuel economy combined with environmental pressures on two-strokes to ensure that the GT550 did not survive the decade.

Above: *Suzuki's 543cc two-stroke triple was a usefully powerful and reliable engine, even if its Ram Air System amounted to no more than a piece of metal that diverted air onto the cylinder head.*

Above left: *Although it wasn't an out and out sports bike, the GT550 was notably slimmer and lighter than Suzuki's three-cylinder flagship, the liquid-cooled GT750.*

Laverda Jota

Laverda's handsome three-cylinder Jota was the most powerful and arguably the fastest of the great Italian superbikes of the 1970s. Powered by a tuned version of the Breganze firm's 981cc dohc three-cylinder engine, it was a big, brutal charger that required plenty of rider input – and rewarded it with breathtaking performance and a spine-tingling exhaust wail.

The Jota resulted from a collaboration between Laverda and Slater Brothers, its UK importer. At Slater's request, Laverda fitted its existing 3C triple with the hot cams and high-compression pistons used by factory endurance racers. Free-breathing pipes completed a 90bhp beast that stormed to a top speed of almost 140mph (225km/h). The tall, heavy triple was prone to high-speed instability but generally handled well, with the help of typically firm Ceriani suspension. Triple Brembo discs gave powerful braking. Numerous production race victories proved that with the right rider, the Jota was the world's fastest superbike.

As a roadster the Jota was demanding. Its vicious acceleration combined with the unfaired riding position, engine vibration and heavy clutch to make every journey an event. In other respects the Laverda was well equipped, with finish and electrics that were excellent by Italian standards. In 1980 Laverda added a half fairing, and in 1982 smoothed the engine by redesigning it with equal, 120-degree firing intervals, in place of the original 180-degree (two pistons up, one down) arrangement. The Jota 120 was more practical and just as fast, although some diehard Jota fans still preferred the uniquely raw and charismatic original.

Above: The Jota demanded a forceful riding style but was capable of fast cornering, as its many production race wins confirmed.

Below: Laverda's big triple was an imposing machine whose performance very much lived up to the muscular look.

Yamaha RD400C

When it screamed onto the market in 1976, Yamaha's RD400C was widely regarded as motorcycling's outstanding middleweight. The two-stroke parallel twin looked good, was reliable, handled well and was relatively inexpensive. Most of all it was fast, racing to just over 100mph (161km/h) and showing a smoking pair of silencers to all its rivals. One US test even described it as: 'the closest thing to a perfect motorcycle that we've ever run up against' and it soon became popular.

Few people were surprised that the RD400C was good, because it was the latest in a line of impressive Yamaha two-stroke twins. The letters RD stood for 'Race Developed'; Yamaha's TZ twins had long dominated the middleweight Grand Prix classes. The RD400C was based on the previous RD350 but featured a major restyle – including angular fuel tank – and comprehensively updated engine and chassis. The enlarged, 398cc reed-valve motor gained rubber mounting, plus many new parts. Its 40bhp peak output was slightly up on rivals' figures, and midrange output was strong.

Performance was predictably thrilling. The Yamaha was half a second quicker than its nearest 400cc rival over a standing quarter mile, and its top speed matched every bike in the class. It handled and stopped well, thanks to firm suspension plus a single brake disc at each end. In 1978 the twin was still popular in updated RD400E form, complete with an extra 4bhp. Tightening emissions laws meant the RD was the last of Yamaha's air-cooled two-stroke twins. It was a brilliant way to end the line.

Above: *The RD400C had a distinctive style thanks to its angular fuel tank, complete with speed-block pattern as used by Yamaha's two-stroke race bikes.*

Below: *Firm suspension helped ensure that the light and agile RD's handling was a good match for its rev-happy straight-line performance.*

Moto Guzzi Le Mans 850

The Le Mans was arguably the most stylish and charismatic of all the great 1970s Italian superbikes. It was certainly one of the fastest. Around the unlikely basis of its transverse V-twin engine, Moto Guzzi fashioned a sports machine that backed up its quintessentially Italian look with exhilarating speed plus outstanding handling and braking. The Le Mans made a magnificent roadster and a useful production racer, and is regarded by many Moto Guzzi fans as the finest bike that the famous old firm has ever produced.

Guzzi created the Le Mans in 1976 by enlarging and tuning the 90-degree, pushrod-operated V-twin engine of the existing 750 S3 roadster – itself a rapid and handsome machine – and adding a bikini fairing, curvaceous petrol tank, uniquely sculpted seat, and paintwork in Italian racing red. Capacity rose to 844cc from the S3's 748cc, the compression ratio was raised, and the motor gained tuning parts including unfiltered Dell'Orto carburettors and free-breathing exhaust. Peak output increased from 72 to 80bhp, and midrange power was also significantly boosted through the rev range.

Straight-line performance was deliciously strong. The big motor was lumpy at low revs, but smoothed and pulled harder through the midrange. The V-twin unit's new-found top-end power gave storming acceleration to a top speed of 130mph (210km/h). Equally addictive was the Le Mans' smooth, relaxed feel which, in combination with the flyscreen's protection, slightly leant-forward riding position and well-padded seat, allowed prolonged high-speed riding in reasonable comfort.

The Le Mans was not the lightest or most agile of superbikes but it handled well, helped by a stiff steel frame and taut suspension. Many '70s superbikes of

Below left: The Le Mans' taut and well-damped suspension helped give handling that was a match for almost every rival superbike, despite its shaft final drive.

Below: With its handlebar fairing, sculpted seat and big, rounded cylinders, Guzzi's flagship had the style to complement its unique brand of high performance.

comparable performance were prone to high-speed weaves, but the V-twin was generally unshakable, and was confidence-inspiring in bends despite the occasionally distracting effect of the shaft final drive. Guzzi's unique linked brake system of three cast-iron Brembo discs was powerful and reliable, too, even in the wet. The handlebar lever operated one front disc; the foot pedal the other plus the rear. Apart from typically poor electrics, the bike was also well built and reliable.

An inevitably high price ensured that the Le Mans did not sell in vast numbers, but Guzzi's flagship boosted the firm's image and gained a strong following. The model remained in production for 19 years, through a series of generally unimpressive updates. The Le Mans Mk2 of 1979 featured an angular full fairing, but was slightly slower. The 1982-model Mk 3 regained some power, but by then the pushrod V-twin had become less competitive. Worse was to follow in 1985 with the curiously styled, 949cc Mk 4, which handled poorly thanks to a 16-inch front wheel introduced without a corresponding change in steering geometry.

The disappointment of the later Le Mans models was heightened by memories of the elegance and competitive performance of the first one. Subsequent V-twins restored some pride to the marque from Mandello del Lario, but it's debatable whether Guzzi or any other firm will build a superbike more stylish and soulful than the original Le Mans 850.

Above: Guzzi's transverse V-twin engine had come a long way since its unlikely beginnings in the firm's tractor-like three-wheeled vehicle of the early 1960s.

Moto Guzzi Le Mans 850 (1976)	
Engine	Air-cooled ohv four-valve pushrod 90-degree transverse V-twin
Capacity	844cc (83 x 78mm)
Maximum power	80bhp at 7300rpm
Transmission	Five-speed, shaft final drive
Frame	Steel spine
Suspension	Telescopic front; twin shocks rear
Brakes	Twin discs front; single disc rear
Weight	476lb (216kg) wet
Top speed	130mph (210km/h)

Triumph T140 Bonneville Silver Jubilee

The Silver Jubilee Bonneville was a rare Triumph success during the 1970s, a decade in which the recently dominant British motorcycle industry was brought to its knees. The original 649cc T120 Bonneville had been one of the stars of the '60s, but had become less competitive by 1973 when its air-cooled, parallel-twin engine was enlarged to 744cc to create the T140 Bonneville. The larger unit produced 52bhp with increased midrange power, and gave the Bonnie extra sales appeal despite some added vibration.

The Silver Jubilee Bonneville was a special edition of the T140, produced in 1977 with Buckingham Palace approval to celebrate Queen Elizabeth II's 25-year reign. It differed from the standard model by having a silver paint scheme with red, white and blue highlights, plus extra chrome on parts including forks, engine covers and rear light. Other changes included a new seat plus wider wheels and tyres. Like the standard model the Jubilee was built in European and US export specification, the latter with higher bars and smaller tank.

Performance was unexceptional but the Bonneville was fun to ride. Its 110mph (177km/h) top speed was less relevant than the twin-cylinder engine's engaging midrange response, and the fine handling delivered by its light and well-suspended chassis. The bike's sales success provided a boost to the workers' co-operative that ran Triumph, having taken control following controversial management plans to close the unprofitable Meriden factory. The Jubilee Bonnie's popularity helped Triumph survive the decade, but the end finally came in 1983.

Below: Silver paintwork was unique to the Jubilee but its 744cc, pushrod-operated parallel-twin engine was identical to that of Triumph's standard T140 Bonneville.

Left: The Bonneville had lost its performance image long before the Silver Jubilee appeared in 1977, but its flexible engine and sweet-handling chassis still made an appealing combination.

Suzuki GS750

ew manufacturers have ever got a completely new motorcycle as close to being absolutely right as Suzuki did in 1977 with the GS750. The firm's first four-stroke superbike was a powerful dohc four that combined stunning straight-line performance with reliability, understated style and sweet handling. It would have been impressive coming from any manufacturer, but given Suzuki's two-stroke background the GS was a massive achievement – albeit one that was heavily influenced by Kawasaki's four-cylinder Z900.

The GS engine shared the Z900's dohc layout, piston diameter and even its valve sizes and timing, reaching its 748cc capacity with a shorter stroke. Peak output was 68bhp, making the Suzuki the most powerful 750 on the market. Chassis design was conventional, based around a well-braced twin-downtube frame that proved notably rigid. Although the front forks and twin rear shocks were of typical design, they were of superior quality and performance to many previous Japanese equivalents. Braking was by single disc front and rear.

Engine performance surpassed anything previously seen from the 750cc class. Crisp low-rev response was matched by strong midrange and a surge of top-end power that sent the Suzuki whirring to a top speed of over 120mph (193km/h). The engine's smoothness and the large dual seat made the GS reasonably comfortable, although the US version's high bars gave a very upright riding position. Handling was outstanding by Japanese standards, combining precise steering with excellent high-speed stability. At a stroke, the GS confirmed Suzuki's arrival as a leading superbike manufacturer.

Above: The GS750's neat, understated styling was a perfect match for its powerful, efficient four-cylinder engine and conventional chassis.

Above left: Suzuki's engineers had undoubtedly been heavily influenced by Kawasaki's Z1 when developing the 748cc GS motor, which shared many of the larger dohc unit's features.

Suzuki GS750 (1977)

Engine Air-cooled dohc eight-valve transverse four

Capacity 749cc (65 x 56.4mm)

Maximum power 68bhp @ 8500rpm

Transmission Five-speed, chain final drive

Frame Steel twin downtube

Suspension Telescopic front; twin shocks rear

Brakes Disc front & rear

Weight 504lb (229kg)

Top speed 125mph (201km/h)

Harley-Davidson XLCR1000 Café Racer

The long, black Café Racer that Harley-Davidson launched in 1977 was the unlikeliest of superbikes. Its basic layout was promising: handlebar fairing, flat bars, big V-twin engine and rearset footrests. Some parts were borrowed from Harley's Sportster, others from the legendary XR750 dirt-tracker. But although the XLCR1000 looked mean and had an undeniable charisma, it was far from the fast, aggressive, Italian-style V-twin charger that its styling suggested.

Its air-cooled, 45-degree V-twin motor came direct from the Sportster, so was a softly-tuned 998cc unit with pushrod valve operation, four-speed gearbox and a peak output of 61bhp. The engine was mounted solidly in a frame that combined a Sportster front end with XR750 components. Forks and shocks were borrowed from the Sportster, though the Café Racer gained a second front disc brake and Goodyear tyres.

The XLCR's basic problem was that, although Harley's traditional engine and chassis technology worked well with a cruiser, it was much less suited to a bike with sporting pretensions. The big V-twin kicked out enough low-down torque to send the Café Racer thundering to 120mph (193km/h). But vibration was a problem even at much slower speeds, and cornering was severely limited by the crude suspension and poor ground clearance. At the time the bike did not appeal either to sporting riders or to Harley's traditional cruiser crowd. These days the verdict is more generous, and the XLCR's style, sound and charisma make up for the fact that it never really was a true Café Racer at all.

Above: The Café Racer's bikini fairing and big V-twin engine gave the look of a racy Italian superbike, but the Harley was a much more laid-back machine.

Above left: Cast-alloy wheels and twin front brake discs were standard fitments, and this XLCR also benefits from a fork brace that added front-end stability.

Yamaha XS750

The good looks, unique format and fine all-round performance of Yamaha's first superbike promised much when the XS750 entered production in 1977. The triple was fast, smooth and comfortable. It handled well and had a distinctive and appealing character. But a variety of mechanical problems, combined with the simultaneous launch of several very capable rivals, ensured that the XS never became the success that its makers had intended.

Yamaha's engineers seemed to have done everything right. The air-cooled, 747cc three-cylinder motor featured twin overhead camshafts, a 120-degree crankshaft and shaft final drive. Its 64bhp peak output was barely down on sportier chain-driven fours, and the motor was both flexible and smooth. The XS cruised effortlessly at high speed, with performance in hand to a top speed of 120mph (193km/h). Handling combined straight-line stability with excellent cornering control, despite the bike's shaft drive system and 512lb (233kg) of weight.

The XS was also comfortable and well detailed, with a roomy riding position, large dual seat, clear instruments and self-cancelling indicators. Magazine testers found very little to criticise apart from the small fuel tank and dim headlight. The competitively priced triple looked set to be a big success – until reports started to circulate of mechanical problems including piston ring failure, seizure of the central cylinder, and gearbox malfunction. Despite Yamaha's attempts to put things right, the damage to the XS750's reputation was done. The triple made little impact on the sales charts, even when uprated in 1980 to create the XS850.

Above: Despite its small fuel tank, the XS750 was an impressively versatile and practical superbike, but its mechanical problems prevented any chance of long-term sales success.

Above: Fine handling was one of the Yamaha's attributes, although the rather heavy triple was an all-rounder rather than a sports machine.

Bimota SB2

It is almost unheard of for a motorcycle to incorporate so many advanced features that all its contemporaries immediately seem dated, but that was the impact of Bimota's SB2 on its launch in 1977. The tiny firm from Rimini – co-founded by a youthful design genius named Massimo Tamburini, and already responsible for world-championship winning Grand Prix racebike chassis – used Suzuki's new 750cc four-cylinder engine to power an exotic superbike that remains arguably the most advanced ever seen.

The SB2 was visually stunning, thanks to a curvaceous, aluminium-lined, glass fibre tank/seat unit that pre-dated current carbon-fibre structures by requiring no rear subframe. The chrome-molybdenum steel frame featuring adjustable steering geometry, heavily braced steering head, and conical couplings that facilitated engine removal. The vertical deCarbon monoshock was worked by a box-section steel swing-arm, which pivoted concentrically to the final-drive sprocket, maintaining constant chain tension. Every component was of premium quality, from the machined alloy triple clamps to the modified Ceriani forks, lightweight cast wheels and drilled Brembo brake discs.

Performance was as mind-blowing as the peerless specification implied. The Bimota's power, aerodynamics and light weight gave searing acceleration to over 130mph (210km/h). The SB2's blend of race-bred geometry, chassis rigidity and suspension control made it remarkably stable and controllable. It also had powerful brakes and abundant ground clearance. Inevitably it was expensive; each of the 70 bikes that Bimota produced cost three times as much as the standard GS750. Few who rode one doubted that the SB2 was worth every bit.

Bimota SB2 (1977)	
Engine	Air-cooled, dohc eight-valve transverse four (Suzuki GS750)
Capacity	749cc (65 x 56.4mm)
Maximum power	68bhp @ 8500rpm (standard engine)
Transmission	Five-speed, chain final drive
Frame	Tubular-steel space frame
Suspension	Telescopic front; monoshock rear
Brakes	Twin discs front; disc rear
Weight	440lb (200kg)
Top speed	130mph (210km/h)

Below: The dramatic one-piece tank/seat unit, fashioned from aluminium-lined glass-fibre, was just one of many high-tech features that made the SB2 by far the most advanced superbike of its day.

Above: The SB2's aerodynamic fairing meant that it was outstandingly fast in a straight line, as well as far superior to almost every other bike in corners.

MV Agusta 850 Magni

MV Agusta fours including the Monza and America were among the fastest and most desirable superbikes of the late 1970s, but even the Italian factory's exotic machines could not match the quality and performance of the race replicas from former race team manager Arturo Magni. After leading MV to 17 consecutive 500cc World Championships, Magni set up an engineering business near his old base at Gallarate, building MV-powered specials fitted with his own engine parts and chassis.

No two Magni-built MVs were identical, but a typical example was powered by a tuned version of the handsome dohc four-cylinder engine, enlarged to 832cc from the America's 789cc and fitted with Arturo's chain drive conversion in place of the original heavy shaft. Hot cams, high-compression pistons and a curvaceous four-pipe exhaust system helped increase power output from the standard 75bhp. Equally important was Magni's frame, which added rigidity by using twin top tubes in place of the standard single spine. Cycle parts were high-class components from firms such as Marzocchi, Koni and Brembo.

The result was a magnificently fast and charismatic roadster that was often fitted with a full fairing to give an authentic Grand Prix replica look. The Magni hurtled towards a top speed of close to 140mph (225km/h), bellowing through its barely silenced exhaust, and cornered with outstanding precision and stability. Inevitably the price of this most exclusive of hand-built race replicas was high. But the Magni's unique blend of performance, character and racing pedigree made every ride a memorable experience.

Above and below: With its yellow No1 plate this Magni resembled one of MV's all-conquering 500cc racers, and its curvaceous exhaust system meant it sounded like one, too. Magni's chain-drive conversion significantly improved handling.

Quasar

The futuristic Quasar was among the best of many attempts over the years to combine the fun of motorcycling with the weather protection of a car. The curious wedge-shaped device, created by Malcolm Newell and Ken Leaman from Bristol in England's West Country, wrapped glass fibre around a tubular-steel framework that enclosed the rider, who sat in a hammock-like seat with feet forward. Car-style luxury features included a cassette player, heater and windscreen wiper, but did not extend to the cramped passenger accommodation.

Requirements for the engine included strong low-rev performance and shaft final drive, which led to the fitment of an 848cc liquid-cooled, pushrod-operated four-cylinder unit from a three-wheeled Reliant car. The softly tuned four produced just 60bhp, but the Quasar's excellent aerodynamics meant that it was capable of 100mph (161km/h) and cruised smoothly and comfortably at close to that speed, its range boosted by impressive fuel economy. Riding the strange machine took some getting used to but in the right hands it could corner rapidly, despite its length and 690lb (314kg) of weight.

Despite its promising all-round performance, the Quasar sold in very small numbers, partly because in 1977 it cost more than twice as much as a 750cc Japanese superbike. Sporadic production continued for several years but fewer than 20 had been built when the marque's second owners hit financial problems in 1982. Original designer Newell updated the concept to create a more powerful successor, the Phasar, based on Kawasaki's Z1300 six, but only a few were produced before the project was abandoned.

Above: The low and slender Quasar's excellent aerodynamics gave it impressive high-speed cruising ability despite its low-powered engine.

Below: Despite being long and heavy, the Quasar could be cornered rapidly, although its unusual handling characteristics meant the roofed bike required a modified riding technique.

Suzuki GS1000

The GS1000 heralded a second generation of Japanese four-cylinder design on its arrival in 1978. Suzuki's first open-class superbike was more powerful and faster than any previous mass-produced four. More importantly, the GS had a strong and sophisticated chassis that not only made it the best handling big bike yet from Japan, but arguably the first whose cornering ability was comparable with that of leading European rivals.

For a machine with such stellar performance the GS1000 had an unspectacular appearance, with restrained styling, slightly raised bars and an air-cooled, 997cc twin-cam engine that resembled those of Suzuki's own GS750 (which had been launched a year earlier) and Kawasaki's Z1000. What was outstanding was the way the motor performed. The GS made 4bhp more power than the benchmark Kawaski, with a maximum of 87bhp. It also developed more torque throughout the range, and was lighter and equally reliable.

A strong, twin-downtube frame held suspension more sophisticated than anything previously seen on a mass-produced roadster. Front forks were air-assisted, and the shocks could be adjusted for rebound damping as well as for the normal preload. Powerful triple disc brakes were marred only by a slight wet-weather delay typical of the time. It added up to a stunning new superbike, as happy scorching smoothly to its 135mph (217km/h) top speed as it was cruising effortlessly or being hustled along a twisty country road. Kawasaki's Z1000, for so long the King, was deposed by a bike that was superior in virtually every respect.

Above: Visually similar to the GS750, the GS1000 combined a strengthened twin-downtube frame design with the most sophisticated suspension yet from a mass-produced four.

Above: Suzuki's 997cc, dohc engine was more powerful than and just as robust as the Kawasaki Z1000 unit that it closely resembled.

Honda CBX1000

The CBX1000 divides opinions like few bikes ever built. In many respects Honda's mighty six was an outstanding superbike. When unleashed in 1978 it was the world's most powerful production machine; a pure-bred sports bike that owed its inspiration to Honda's fabulous multi-cylinder racers of the 1960s, and whose chassis was boosted by innovative use of lightweight materials. But the expensive CBX sold poorly and was soon dropped from Honda's range.

Its heritage was certainly an inspiration for the bike's project leader Shoichiro Irimajiri, who as a young engineer in the 1960s had worked on the high-revving multi-cylinder Honda Grand Prix bikes ridden to world titles by stars including Mike Hailwood. Race-bred technology was used to design the dohc cylinder head, which held 24 tiny valves. The CBX was innovative in its use of magnesium for some engine covers, and the powerplant featured a hollow exhaust camshaft for further weight reduction.

Neat engine details included a jackshaft, above the gearbox, which drove the alternator and ignition system. This allowed the 1047cc motor to be very narrow at its base. Legroom was provided for the rider by tilting the cylinders forward by 33 degrees, and by angling the six carburettors inwards in two banks of three. Maximum output was 105bhp at 9000rpm.

Styling was dramatic, emphasised by the way in which the massively broad engine, which being air-cooled required no radiator, was suspended by the tubular-steel frame. The absence of downtubes added to the impact of a machine that was rare in being designed as a no-compromise sports machine, at a time when much of Honda's focus was on the touring-oriented US market.

Straight-line performance was majestic, combining shoulder-splitting acceleration with remarkable six-cylinder smoothness. At low revs the CBX

Above: Honda suspended the CBX engine from its frame in order to keep the dramatic bank of six air-cooled cylinders in full view, adding greatly to the bike's visual appeal.

Honda CBX1000 (1978)	
Engine	Air-cooled dohc 24-valve six
Capacity	1047cc (64.5 x 53.4mm)
Maximum power	105bhp @ 9000rpm
Transmission	Five-speed, chain final drive
Frame	Tubular-steel
Suspension	Telescopic front; twin shocks rear
Brakes	Twin discs front; disc rear
Weight	572lb (260kg) wet
Top speed	135mph (217km/h)

Left: For such a big, wide bike the CBX handled very well, thanks to firm suspension and Honda's attempts to save weight by innovative use of aluminium and magnesium.

responded obediently and without fuss. When the rev-counter needle reached 6000rpm the bike came alive, leaping towards its 135mph (217km/h) top speed with a high-pitched howl from its exhaust.

Handling was excellent for a big machine that scaled 572lb (260kg) despite Honda's attempts to save weight by using aluminium handlebars, plastic mudguards and magnesium engine covers. Suspension was reasonably firm and well-damped, stability was good, and the bike also slowed reliably thanks to a capable twin-disc front brake.

The glamorous Six generated a storm of publicity on both sides of the Atlantic, much of it favourable. But sales were disappointing, especially in the US. Some motorcyclists were wary of its relatively untried technology, but for many the main drawback was price. The CBX was typically 50 per cent more expensive than comparable fours, yet its performance advantage was minimal.

Honda had no more joy with the fully faired CBX1000B, introduced in 1981. Aimed at touring riders, it also sold slowly. The bold six-cylinder gamble had failed but the Six had given Honda's image a much needed boost. Years later it retains a cult following, based on the unique way that it combined style, technology and performance. Few people would conclude that the CBX was a success, but the two-wheeled world would have been much less interesting without it.

Below: This immaculate CBX is fitted with the accessory engine bars that helped protect its wide engine in a crash. The high price and running costs contributed to the fast and stylish Honda's commercial failure.

Yamaha XS1100

The XS1100, launched in 1978, was a Japanese superbike of the old school: a big, powerful engine in a big, heavy chassis. Its black-finished 1101cc four-cylinder motor was tuned for flexibility rather than outright power, and produced 95bhp with massive low-rev torque. Technically conventional, with twin camshafts opening two valves per cylinder, it followed Yamaha's earlier XS750 triple in using shaft final drive, and was notably more reliable.

Even with as little as 50mph (80km/h) showing on the square-shaped speedometer, a tweak of the throttle was enough to send the Yamaha storming forward with almost enough force to bend its handlebars. Top speed was over 130mph (209km/h) but the bike was better suited to relatively gentle cruising. Its steel twin-cradle frame was heavily braced but the XS could not hide the fact that it weighed almost 600lb (273kg) with fuel. High-speed stability was often marginal and sometimes distinctly worrying. In slow bends the four was merely ponderous.

The XS1100 was fairly comfortable, despite its high handlebars, thanks mainly to the engine's smoothness and the generous seat. With useful details such as a big tank, fuel gauge and self-cancelling indicators, it was well equipped, too. The XS was at its best when ridden gently on a long straight freeway, loaded with luggage and fitted with a big fairing, and became popular with touring riders in the US. Elsewhere it was less successful, although Yamaha prolonged its life into the 1980s with the mean looking XS1100 Sport, featuring a handlebar fairing, smaller fuel tank and black paintwork.

Above and below: The XS1100 was too big and heavy to be popular in many countries, but its straight-line performance earned admirers in the United States. This Yamaha's high bars and short exhaust system confirm that it is a machine designed for the US market.

Ducati Darmah SD

The stylish, rapid and versatile Darmah turned plenty of heads when it was introduced in 1977 as a successor to Ducati's relatively unsuccessful 860GT and GTS tourers. Shaped by Italjet boss and former Ducati works racer Leo Tartarini, the Darmah had a much more modern look, with its rounded tank flowing gracefully into its seat and tailpiece. The Darmah – named after a tiger in a children's book – had plenty of bite, too, thanks to an 864cc desmodromic V-twin that was a detuned version of Ducati's racy 900SS unit.

Smaller carburettors and a restrictive exhaust system limited the original Darmah's appeal so the following year Ducati created the Darmah SD by fitting 900SS-style Dell'Ortos and loud Conti pipes. The new bike's peak output of about 60bhp (Ducati didn't quote precise figures) was still modest, and the bike's 115mph (185km/h) maximum speed was well down on that of the Super Sport. But the Darmah scored with its V-twin character and flexible power delivery, which allowed effortless cruising.

The Darmah also upheld Ducati's reputation for fine handling, thanks to its stiff ladder frame, well-damped suspension and excellent brakes and tyres. Unfortunately, it also upheld a less welcome Bolognese tradition relating to build quality and reliability. The Darmah's chrome and paintwork were poor, its electrics were untrustworthy and its engine was expensive to maintain. An on-form Darmah was a great all-rounder: quick, stable and enjoyable to ride. But touring riders demanded practicality, and the Darmah did not deliver enough to become the success that financially struggling Ducati badly needed.

Above: The 864cc bevel-drive desmo V-twin was impressively flexible, but unfortunately the Darmah's unreliability and poor build quality limited its appeal.

Honda CB900F

The CB900F was evidence of a renewed commitment to four-cylinder superbikes by Honda, whose sales and image had suffered during the 1970s due to the firm's failure to develop a dohc four to match Kawasaki's Z1 and its followers. When the CB900F was launched in 1979 its sporty nature was clear from its lean 'Eurostyle' shape, low handlebars and semi-rearset footrests. This machine, Honda announced, was inspired by the firm's 1000cc RCB racers, which had dominated endurance events including the Bol d'Or 24 hours in recent years.

Its 901cc twin-cam engine held 16 valves and produced an impressive 94bhp, but had long-stroke dimensions and was tuned for midrange acceleration rather than top-end power. The Honda's flexible delivery helped make it effortlessly fast, and the leant-forward riding position and wide seat made it comfortable at most speeds, en route to a maximum of over 130mph (209km/h). Handling was excellent, too. The four-into-two exhaust, and the use of plastic for parts including the front mudguard, helped keep weight to 512lb (233kg). Suspension worked well, with the multi-adjustable shocks giving a taut and controlled ride.

Stopping power was less impressive, and braking was uprated in 1982, when a revised model appeared featuring twin-piston front calipers plus Honda's TRAC anti-dive system. The CB900F also developed a reputation for dubious reliability, with its cam chain being a particular weakness. But it did a reasonable job of restoring Honda's image for four-cylinder performance, and was also fitted with a fairing to create the capable CB900F2 tourer.

Above: The CB900F's Eurostyle look was reminiscent of Honda's smaller CB400 and 250 twins, but the big four's performance put it in a very different league.

Honda CB900F (1979)

Engine Air-cooled dohc 16-valve transverse four

Capacity 901cc (64.5 x 69mm)

Maximum power 95bhp @ 9000rpm

Transmission Five-speed, chain final drive

Frame Steel twin downtube

Suspension Telescopic front; twin shocks rear

Brakes Twin discs front; disc rear

Weight 513lb (233kg)

Top speed 135mph (217km/h)

Kawasaki Z1300

The arrival of Kawasaki's gigantic, controversial Z1300 six in 1979 provided a perfect final chapter for the remarkable motorcycling story of the 1970s. Superbikes had been getting bigger, more powerful, heavier and more complex throughout the decade, but there had been nothing to compare with the Z1300, which pushed the envelope in every direction. Its enormous 1286cc six-cylinder engine produced 120bhp, making it the world's most powerful streetbike by a clear 15bhp. Despite having no fairing, the Z1300 weighed 670lb (305kg) with fuel, and added the complexity of liquid-cooling and shaft final drive to its engine's dohc, 12-valve specification.

Its large radiator meant the slab-sided Kawasaki gained little visual impact from its engine layout. A massive steel frame and well-chosen suspension at least meant that it had improbably good handling to match its searing acceleration. It whistled to its 135mph (216km/h) top speed without a wobble, was stable even in fast curves, and had efficient brakes and tyres. But the bike's exposed riding position and forward-set footrests meant its rider struggled to exploit the engine's effortless high-speed ability. And although the Six was smooth, its snatchy throttle response and busy feel did not make for particularly relaxed riding.

Despite its unmatched power, size and complexity, the Kawasaki offered nothing that several smaller and simpler bikes could not provide. The expensive Z1300 sold slowly and marked the end of the Japanese manufacturer's apparent belief that bigger was better. But it gained a cult status and remained in production, with few changes, until 1989.

Above: The giant six-cylinder Kawasaki's conventional styling and a modest twin-silencer exhaust system meant that in isolation it looked almost ordinary.

Above: For such a huge bike the Z1300 went round corners surprisingly well, thanks to well-chosen geometry, a massively strong frame and suitably firm suspension.

Chapter 5

The 1980s

Suzuki GSX1100

As the 1980s began, the arrival of Suzuki's GSX1100 represented another step in the evolution of the previous decade's classic Japanese superbike with its air-cooled, four-cylinder engine and twin rear shock absorbers. An unusual headlight design and rather bulbous styling meant the GSX was not the most stylish of bikes. But its 1075cc, 16-valve powerplant added both midrange and top-end performance to Suzuki's previous GS1000 unit, and the GSX's chassis also highlighted Suzuki's ability to refine an already successful design.

The GSX engine used Suzuki's new Twin Swirl Combustion Chamber cylinder head design to produce a maximum of 100bhp, with notably strong delivery throughout the range. The twin-downtube steel frame incorporated no obvious high technology, but it was admirably strong and held sophisticated suspension with adjustable rebound damping at both ends. The result was a bike that had a wonderfully flexible power delivery, cruised smoothly at 90mph (145km/h), and charged towards a top speed approaching 140mph (225km/h) with a force that left its rider struggling to hang on.

The GSX weighed over 550lb (250kg) with fuel and couldn't match the manoeuvrability of some lighter superbikes, but it handled and braked remarkably well for such a big machine. Its broad seat helped make it reasonably comfortable despite the exposed riding position, and it also proved as reliable as its GS1000 predecessor. A new generation of faired, liquid-cooled, monoshock machines was on the way, but the GSX1100 proved that in 1980 the familiar format of a naked, air-cooled, twin-shock four still produced the fastest and best superbike.

Above: Suzuki's big fours had always handed well, and the GSX was the best yet thanks to its strong steel frame and sophisticated, adjustable suspension components at both ends.

Left: The GSX1100's most obvious innovation was its rectangular headlight, but the more important new feature was the 16-valve cylinder head design that gave Suzuki's dohc four-cylinder engine a new level of performance.

Suzuki GSX1100 (1981)	
Engine Air-cooled dohc 16-valve transverse four	
Capacity 1075cc (72 x 66mm)	
Maximum power 100bhp @ 8700rpm	
Transmission Five-speed, chain final drive	
Frame Steel twin downtube	
Suspension Telescopic front; twin shocks rear	
Brakes Twin discs front; disc rear	
Weight 554lb (252kg) wet	
Top speed 137mph (220km/h)	

BMW R80 G/S

BMW opened up a whole new world with the launch of the R80 G/S in 1980. By taking one of its large-capacity flat-twin engines, and using it to power an enduro-styled machine designed for use both on- and off-road, the German marque sparked a craze for big dual-purpose bikes that would expand over the next three decades, leading to rival models from many manufacturers.

The G/S initials stood for Gelände, German for off-road, and Strasse, meaning street – and the BMW was a handy performer on both. Its engine was a 797cc version of the familiar air-cooled, pushrod-operated boxer, and was notable for its coated aluminium cylinder bores and single-plate diaphragm clutch. Its 49bhp peak output gave punchy acceleration, reasonably smooth cruising and a top speed of 105mph (169km/h). Equally important was the sound handling, on rough or smooth surfaces, which resulted from the G/S's high quality suspension and relatively light weight, plus an innovative single-sided monoshock and drive shaft arrangement that allowed rapid rear wheel removal.

The stylish, rugged and versatile G/S made a fine road bike and a very capable off-roader. It became very popular, boosted by four victories in the Paris-Dakar Rally in the early 1980s. BMW responded by developing a special Paris-Dakar version of the roadster, available as a kit or complete bike, and in 1987 enlarged the engine to 980cc, creating the R100GS. Further updates would see the GS go from strength to strength, providing opportunities for two-wheeled adventure to thousands of riders in the process.

Above: With its lean enduro styling and long-travel suspension the G/S was very different to BMW's previous boxer twins, and its versatility soon made it popular.

Above: Belgian star Gaston Rahier rode this heavily modified G/S to his second Paris-Dakar victory in 1985, as BMW dominated by winning four of the first seven Rallies.

Moto Guzzi V1000 Convert

*oto Guzzi's V1000 Convert was one of the big touring V-twins that headed the marque's range into the early 1980s, when its sportier models had become less competitive due largely to lack of investment. With its slow-revving, 949cc engine combined with an automatic gearbox, the Convert provided an even more laid-back ride than the California, its more conventional sibling, which had been one of Guzzi's most popular models since its launch in the early '70s.

The Convert was an attempt to broaden the California's appeal still further, especially in the US, where automatic cars were commonplace and automatic bikes looked to have potential. Guzzi's engineers enlarged the California's engine from 844cc to 949cc and replaced the five-speed gearbox with a hydraulic torque converter and two-speed box. Peak output was 71bhp, slightly up on the California's 68bhp. The chassis was similar to that of the conventional model, featuring Guzzi's own forks and linked, triple-disc brake system.

The torque converter worked well, helping give the V1000 a relaxed character, effortless high-speed cruising ability and 110mph (177km/h) top speed. Handling was typically stable, though the Convert required a slightly different riding style due to its lack of engine braking, which put more emphasis on the powerful Brembo system. The V1000 made a capable and comfortable tourer, especially when fitted with the screen and panniers that came as standard in some markets. But the slightly quicker, more economical and similarly priced California was more popular, and remained in Guzzi's range long after Convert production had ended.

Above: Guzzi's air-cooled, transverse V-twin engine looked familiar but was modified with enlarged 949cc capacity and a hydraulic torque converter in place of the gearbox.

Below: The Convert was visually very similar to Guzzi's conventional T3 roadster, and was often modified with touring-related factory accessories including screen and panniers.

Kawasaki GPz1100

The GPz1100 arrived at high speed in 1981 to restore Kawasaki's faded reputation for red-blooded performance. Its format was very much that of a traditional big Kawasaki four, though the GPz added the refinement of fuel injection to the familiar blend of air-cooled, two-valves-per-cylinder engine and steel-framed, twin-shock chassis. With its scarlet paintwork and angular styling, it was a muscular-looking machine that weighed-in at a hefty 561lb (255kg) with fuel, and was closely related to its predecessor the Z1000H.

Kawasaki's engineers enlarged the litre-bike's engine to 1089cc, and tuned it with bigger valves, hotter cams, high-compression pistons and a lightened crankshaft. Its 108bhp maximum output gave the GPz a horsepower advantage over every rival four in 1981, though not over Kawasaki's own Z1300 six. Its chassis was based on that of the Z1000H, with larger-diameter frame tubes, revised geometry and uprated suspension including damping-adjustable shocks.

The result was not a particularly sophisticated superbike, but it was a phenomenally fast and exhilarating one. The GPz combined vicious acceleration with a top speed of 140mph (225km/h), and also had excellent low-rev throttle response. Handling was generally good for such a big naked bike, although the Kawasaki was prone to twitch when pushed really hard in bends. Its brakes were powerful, the big motor was unburstable, and the rapid red GPz did much to put Kawasaki's big fours back in the spotlight. By 1983 the GPz1100 had gained a half fairing and monoshock suspension, confirming the marque's return to form.

Above: The GPz was a striking looking machine, with angular styling, red paintwork, and a black-finished engine and exhaust system.

Below: Cornering performance was acceptable but aggressive riding revealed the limitations of the big, heavy Kawasaki's chassis.

Yamaha RD350LC

Yamaha's line of fast and exciting two-stroke middleweights was taken to a new level in the early '80s by the introduction of the RD350LC, which added the sophistication of liquid cooling to the air-cooled RD model's parallel-twin engine layout. The LC was developed from outstanding air-cooled two-stroke roadsters including the RD350 and RD400, using input from Yamaha's all-conquering liquid-cooled TZ250 and 350 racers.

Despite its liquid cooling system, the LC's 347cc engine owed more to that of the RD400 roadster than to the TZ350 racer. Its water jacket maintained a constant temperature and allowed the engine to be in a higher state of tune without loss of reliability. Liquid cooling also helped make the 47bhp motor cleaner and quieter than its air-cooled predecessor, important for environmental reasons although not enough to allow it to be sold in the US.

The 350LC's main chassis innovation was to replace the air-cooled model's twin shocks with a TZ-style cantilever rear suspension system, with a diagonally mounted monoshock under the seat. The rest of the chassis was conventional, with a twin-downtube steel frame, slightly raised bars and twin-disc front brake. The similarly styled RD250LC, launched at the same time, produced 35bhp and was most easily distinguishable by its single disc.

Above: *Despite its wide, slightly raised handlebars the RD350LC was a pure-bred sports bike.*

Below: *The Yamaha's specification incorporated race-developed features including twin front disc brakes, liquid-cooled two-stroke engine and monoshock rear suspension.*

Of all the larger LC's attributes, its power delivery was the most addictive. The motor was well behaved and docile at low revs, and it idled reliably after starting with a gentle kick. But when the rev-counter hit 6000rpm the bike came alive, surging towards its 110mph (177km/h) top speed with an exhilarating burst of acceleration and a piercing two-stroke scream.

Provided it was kept on the boil with frequent use of the six-speed box, the little two-stroke could show a smoky pair of pipes to the riders of much bigger bikes. The Yamaha's forks were slightly soft, particularly when the powerful front brake was used hard. But the frame was strong, the rear suspension worked well and the lightweight LC, which weighed just 330lb (150kg) with fuel, combined light, precise steering with impressive stability for such a racy machine.

Its agility and speed combined to make the RD350LC superbly exciting to ride, and a competitive price helped make it hugely popular. It was fast, reliable (even when tuned, usually), agile, reasonably practical, tuneable, raceable, and, most of all, brilliant fun. Its popularity was boosted by a starring role in a televised one-make race series, first in Britain and later internationally, in which standard 350LCs produced some thrillingly close and spectacular racing.

The LC earned lasting cult status as the ultimate poor boy's superbike. Over the years it was updated several times, notably in 1983 to produce the RD350 YPVS or 'Power Valve', nicknamed after its midrange-boosting exhaust power valve. Eventually the two-stroke was killed off by emission laws, but not before it had brought fast and furious fun to a generation of riders.

Yamaha RD350LC (1981)	
Engine	Liquid-cooled two-stroke parallel twin
Capacity	347cc (64 x 54mm)
Maximum power	47bhp @ 8500rpm
Transmission	Six-speed, chain final drive
Frame	Steel twin downtube
Suspension	Telescopic front; single shock rear
Brakes	Twin discs front; drum rear
Weight	309lb (141kg)
Top speed	110mph (177km/h)

Below: The 350LC's light weight, agile handling and abundant ground clearance combined with its rev-happy straight-line performance to make the two-stroke fast and hugely entertaining.

Honda CB1100R

The magnificent CB1100R was a uniquely fast and refined machine that showed what Honda's engineers could do when designing a high-performance superbike with little regard for cost. Launched in 1981, primarily to win high-level production races including Australia's Castrol Six-Hour, the CB1100R was based on Honda's CB900F. The air-cooled, 16-valve engine was enlarged to 1062cc and uprated with modifications including increased compression ratio, plus stronger conrods and bottom end. Peak power was increased to 115bhp, the highest yet figure from a production four.

Honda also refined the CB900F's steel-framed chassis format to new levels of sophistication. The frame tubes were strengthened, and held the most advanced suspension yet seen on a streetbike: front forks with air assistance, and twin rear shocks with adjustable compression and rebound damping, plus remote fluid reservoirs to resist overheating. The equally innovative front brake incorporated twin-piston calipers and big twin discs.

The CB1100R was fitted with a half fairing and single seat, and proved every bit as fast and capable as it looked. Its engine was flexible, smooth and powerful enough for a top speed of 145mph (233km/h). Handling, braking and ground clearance were exceptional. The small numbers built were quickly sold despite costing roughly 75 per cent more than the CB900F, and the exotic 1100R justified its price by proving almost unbeatable on the track.

Above: The original, 1981-model CB1100R's half fairing and single seat were changed for a full fairing and dual-seat the following year, but the Honda kept its unbeatable blend of tuned, 1062cc four-cylinder engine, rigid steel frame and premium quality cycle parts.

Honda CB1100R (1981)

Engine Air-cooled dohc 16-valve transverse four

Capacity 1062cc (70 x 69mm)

Maximum power 115bhp @ 9000rpm

Transmission Five-speed, chain final drive

Frame Steel twin downtube

Suspension Telescopic front; twin shocks rear

Brakes Twin discs front; disc rear

Weight 518lb (235kg) dry

Top speed 142mph (228km/h)

Hesketh V1000

When the Hesketh V1000 was launched in 1981 it was billed by its maker, Lord Alexander Hesketh, as the superbike that would relaunch the British motorcycle industry. The V1000 combined a powerful 992cc V-twin engine with a top-class chassis, and was hand built in limited numbers to be the finest superbike money could buy. Assembled in a workshop in the grounds of Hesketh's Northamptonshire mansion, it was intended as a modern-day Vincent; a stylish, rapid and fine-handling roadburner that proved the British could still build motorcycles of the highest quality.

Hesketh was a wealthy aristocrat who had run a successful Formula One racecar team, and his handsome V1000 was undoubtedly promising. Its air-cooled, 992cc 90-degree V-twin engine, designed by four-stroke specialists Weslake, used twin cams and four valves per cylinder to produce an impressive 86bhp. The frame was a neat structure of nickel-plated steel tubing, and held high-quality components including Marzocchi suspension and Brembo disc brakes.

The V1000's performance gave some reasons for optimism. The Hesketh was reasonably fast and smooth, with a relaxed cruising feel and top speed of 120mph (193km/h). Although heavy, at 506lb (230kg), it handled and braked very well. But, as well as being noisy and unreliable, the engine leaked oil and had an unacceptably poor transmission.

Production was delayed, faults were slow to be corrected, losses mounted, and Hesketh Motorcycles went bust in May 1992. The following year Lord Alexander set up a new firm to produce a fully faired touring version of the V-twin, the Vampire, but built few bikes before abandoning motorcycles for good.

Hesketh V1000 (1975)	
Engine	Air-cooled dohc eight-valve 90-degree V-twin
Capacity	992cc (95 x 70mm)
Maximum power	86bhp at 6500rpm
Transmission	Five-speed, chain final drive
Frame	Tubular steel
Suspension	Telescopic front; twin shocks rear
Brakes	Twin discs front; single disc rear
Weight	506lb (230kg) wet
Top speed	120mph (193km/h)

Below: The V1000 was a stylish superbike whose V-twin engine layout, high-quality cycle parts and British origin drew inevitable comparisons with Vincent's Rapide of the 1950s.

Above: Hesketh's shiny nickel-plated frame held a powerful 992cc V-twin engine, but problems of excessive noise, oil leaks, unreliability and poor transmission proved impossible to overcome.

Ducati Pantah

The Pantah's impact lasted long after the sweet-running Ducati middleweight's heyday in the early 1980s. It was the Pantah's air-cooled V-twin engine, with belt drive to single overhead camshafts, that started a vital new chapter in Ducati's history. Not only did the Pantah 500 and its 583cc successor help revive the Bologna firm's fortunes by becoming successful in their own right, but their engine design formed the basis of the models that followed.

Fabio Taglioni, the legendary chief engineer who designed the Pantah, used the experience he had gained on Ducati's early-1970s 500cc V-twin Grand Prix racer, which featured toothed cam belts, to design a similar roadgoing system that was cheap, quiet and reliable. The initial Pantah, launched in 1979, had a 499cc engine that produced 52bhp. That output increased to 58bhp for the Pantah 600, which followed in 1981 and featured an unchanged tubular-steel ladder frame, plus tall half fairing, large dual seat and high-quality cycle parts from specialists including Marzocchi and Brembo.

The Pantah was slightly more refined and rider-friendly than many previous Ducatis. The 600, in particular, was quick, surging towards a top speed of close to 120mph (193km/h) with impressive acceleration. It also handled superbly, aided by taut suspension and only 415lb (188kg) of weight. Equally importantly, its smoothness and relatively efficient exhaust gave a sophisticated feel without losing Ducati's traditional character. Although expensive by middleweight standards, the Pantah helped Ducati survive a difficult financial time, before being developed to create the bigger models on which the marque's continued recovery was based.

Above: *Two years after the launch of the original 499cc Pantah, Ducati launched the Pantah 600 featuring a more powerful engine and subtly reshaped bodywork.*

Above: *Handling was one of the Pantah's great assets, thanks to its light weight, rigid steel trellis frame and firm, well-damped suspension components.*

Laverda Montjuic Mk2

There has arguably never been a more single-minded, antisocial motorcycle from a major manufacturer than the Laverda Montjuic of the early 1980s. The bright orange 497cc parallel twin, named after Barcelona's city centre circuit (where Laverdas had raced successfully) was the ultimate 'brain-out' bike: an aggressive single-seat sportster with a racy riding position, tuned engine, unfiltered carbs, deafening exhaust system, and total lack of civility or compromise. It was essentially a modified version of Laverda's Alpino 500 roadster, and was inspired by the Formula racebikes that the Italian firm had developed for a one-make racing series.

Numerous engine tuning parts increased the dohc twin's output to about 50bhp, and the free-breathing Montjuic engine could be revved through its redline to 9500rpm – until, occasionally, it blew up in expensive fashion. Brembo's disc brakes gave powerful stopping, and the Montjuic's light weight, strong tubular-steel frame and firm Marzocchi suspension helped give taut and responsive handling, although the handlebar fairing often triggered a slight weave as the Laverda bellowed towards its top speed of about 110mph (177km/h).

Laverda addressed the instability with the Montjuic Mk2, which was introduced in 1982 featuring a slightly larger, frame-mounted fairing and a one-piece seat/sidepanel unit. High-speed handling was improved, and the majority of the Montjuics exported were Mk2s. In terms of pure performance, the Laverda failed to live up to its racy image and high price. But for owners who appreciated its snarling character, the Montjuic was a wonderfully involving bike to ride.

Above: *The Montjuic's straight-line performance was disappointing for such an exotic machine, but there was no doubting the cornering ability provided by the Laverda's rigid frame and taut suspension.*

Above left: *The Montjuic Mk2's frame-mounted half fairing cured the original model's high-speed instability without compromising the middleweight twin's uniquely raw and aggressive character.*

Honda CX500 Turbo

onda's huge and complex CX500 Turbo was like no bike seen before when it arrived in all its fully faired splendour in 1982. Previous turbocharged bikes had been specials, built for ultimate straight-line performance with little regard for cost or longevity. For the world's largest manufacturer to develop a production turbo-bike was a radical departure – and the engine that Honda chose to use made the project even more remarkable.

The basic CX500 was an unglamorous middleweight all-rounder, powered by a 497cc liquid-cooled, 80-degree transverse V-twin engine. That hardly made it ideal as a basis for turbocharging, the system of exhaust-driven forced induction that is best suited to the regular power impulses of a big, multi-cylinder engine. In fact the pushrod-operated V-twin was almost the least suitable powerplant imaginable. Cynics suggested that the bike was intended more as a statement of Honda's engineering prowess than a serious motorcycle.

The CX engine's size meant that it required the world's smallest turbocharger. Built by specialists IHI to Honda's specification, its blades measured less than two inches (5cm) in diameter and spun at 200,000rpm. Many engine components were uprated to cope. A stronger crankshaft, clutch and conrods, plus Honda's first production-specification forged pistons, helped withstand the increase in peak power output from 50bhp to the Turbo's 82bhp.

Honda put almost as much effort into the rest of the bike as into the engine, for the Turbo highlighted technology including a digital ignition and fuel-injection system, twin-piston brake calipers, TRAC anti-dive, and Pro-Link single-shock rear suspension. Its most striking feature was the fairing, complete with integral indicators and a sophisticated instrument console containing a turbo-boost gauge, clock and fuel gauge.

The fairing was outstandingly efficient, combining with the broad seat to allow high-speed cruising in comfort. But the Honda's straight-line performance was modest by superbike standards, with sluggish acceleration and a top speed of

Below left: The Turbo's comprehensive instrument panel included a boost gauge, between the main dials, as well as a fuel gauge and digital clock.

Below: The Honda's neatly shaped fairing combined with the broad dual seat to give an unmistakable look and make the Turbo a comfortable grand tourer.

125mph (201km/h). Equally disappointingly – and predictably, given its engine layout – the CX suffered from turbo lag, the delay between throttle opening and engine response that made precise control difficult.

Given the limitations presented by its engine layout, the CX500 Turbo was in many ways a fine grand tourer. It cruised at speed with a stable and long-legged feel, and handled and braked well for a bike that weighed almost 600lb (273kg) with fuel. But for all Honda's clever engineering, the bike could not fully overcome the drawbacks inherent in its complexity and weight. Its inevitably high price ensured that relatively few were sold.

A year later Honda uprated it by producing the CX650 Turbo, which was better and more exciting due to reduced turbo lag and the extra horsepower that gave arm-wrenching acceleration and a top speed of 135mph (217km/h). But even this more powerful Turbo was still no quicker than many simpler and cheaper bikes, and remained in production for only a year. The other three Japanese manufacturers each produced a short-lived turbo model before motorcycling's turbocharging revolution ran out of breath in the late 1980s.

Honda CX500 Turbo (1982)

Engine	Liquid-cooled ohv pushrod four-valve 80-degree turbocharged transverse V-twin
Capacity	497cc (78 x 52mm)
Maximum power	82bhp @ 8000rpm
Transmission	Five-speed, shaft final drive
Frame	Steel spine
Suspension	Telescopic front; single shock rear
Brakes	Twin discs front; disc rear
Weight	527lb (240kg)
Top speed	125mph (201km/h)

Above: Despite being wide enough to hide the cylinders of its transverse V-twin engine when viewed from the front, the Turbo was very aerodynamically efficient.

Suzuki GSX1100S Katana

The Katana scythed onto the scene in 1982 to show that a Japanese firm could produce a bold and imaginatively styled superbike. Ironically the Katana, named after a Japanese ceremonial sword, was shaped in Germany by the Target Design styling house that had created BMW's R90S. Around Suzuki's excellent but bland-looking GSX1100, Target fashioned an aggressive sportster with a flyscreen, clip-on bars and swooping tank-seat section.

The Katana looked fast when standing still, and had the performance to match. Tuning the GSX's 1075cc air-cooled, 16-valve motor increased peak output by 11bhp to 111bhp. The twin-cradle frame was retained, but new triple clamps gave increased stability. The forks were fitted with hydraulic anti-dive, Suzuki's latest Grand-Prix developed extra; the shocks gained stiffer springs.

Straight-line performance was similar to the GSX's, with smooth, strong midrange acceleration to a top speed of over 140mph (225km/h). At high speeds the Katana's low bars and rearset footpegs combined with the flyscreen to improve aerodynamics and wind protection. At almost 550lb (250kg) the Katana was heavy but its frame and firm suspension were well up to hard cornering, and the triple disc brakes were powerful.

Inevitably there were compromises. The racy riding position was impractical in town, the narrow bars and conservative geometry gave heavy steering, and the seat was uncomfortable. But the Suzuki's looks, speed and competitive price combined to make it a big success. It gained a cult following, inspired numerous other Katana models, and years later was put back in production, barely changed, for the Japanese market.

Above and below: The Katana's combination of strong steel frame and firm suspension gave excellent handling, but the Suzuki's main attraction was its integrated styling, from the sharp fairing nose and flyscreen to the neatly blended sidepanels and seat.

Kawasaki Z1100R

The lime-green Z1100R was a four-cylinder superbike of the old school, built to celebrate factory race ace Eddie Lawson's back-to-back US Superbike titles at the start of the decade. With its high handlebars, two-valves-per-cylinder air-cooled engine and twin-shock rear suspension, the Z1100R was an unlikely race replica. But its blend of simple style, somewhat crude performance and racing pedigree held an undeniable appeal, and breathed new life into Kawasaki's classical 1970s format.

Kawasaki fans in the US had already been offered a mean green 'Lawson Replica' four when the Z1100R was launched in 1984. But enthusiasts in other markets had been disappointed by the firm's Z1000J, which had white paint and mediocre performance. The Z1100R not only featured more appropriate green paintwork, but its engine was enlarged to 1089cc, increasing peak output to 114bhp. Kawasaki also made an extra effort with the chassis, which featured a Lawson-style bikini fairing plus similarly authentic-looking contoured saddle and gold-finished Kayaba remote-reservoir shocks.

The Z1100R could not match the searing performance or sophistication of Kawasaki's new liquid-cooled GPZ900R but the air-cooled four generated plenty of speed and excitement. Its flexible power deliver provided storming midrange acceleration and a top speed of over 140mph (225km/h). The handlebar fairing triggered some high-speed instability but handling was generally sound, and the Kawasaki's brakes were powerful. Behind its aggressive image the big four was an improbably versatile all-rounder. As the new-generation GPZ900R pointed towards motorcycling's future, the Z1100R was an exhilarating blast from the past.

Above: To superbike fans of the mid-'80s, a big green Kawasaki four with a bikini fairing was instantly evocative of Eddie Lawson's US championship-winning racebike.

Below: This Z1100R adds an aftermarket four-into-one exhaust system to the standard Kawasaki's racer-inspired features including bikini fairing, stepped seat and Kayaba remote-reservoir shocks.

BMW K100RS

The introduction of BMW's K-series fours in 1984 was a pivotal moment in the firm's long history. The German marque had been known for air-cooled singles and boxer twins for more than half a century but sales in most markets were poor, and the range was in need of a boost. It came in unexpected fashion with a distinctive trio of bikes – the K100 roadster, K100RS sports-tourer and K100RT tourer – that held their 987cc, dohc liquid-cooled engines with four cylinders horizontally, facilitating shaft final drive to the rear wheel.

Pick of the bunch was arguably the K100RS, whose angular half fairing gave useful wind protection that the naked K100 lacked, without the bulk of the taller K100RT. Many parts were shared between all three models, including the fuel-injected, long-stroke engine, which had a strong midrange output and a respectable maximum of 90bhp. With a steel-framed chassis, telescopic forks and single rear suspension unit the BMW's chassis was fairly conventional, and its solid construction contributed to a weight of over 550lb (250kg) with fuel.

Performance of the naked K100 was modest by Japanese four-cylinder standards, but the similar K100RS gained considerably from the extra comfort and stability provided by its fairing. It had a broad spread of power, was good for 135mph (217km/h) and cruised effortlessly, if not particularly smoothly, at speed. Handling was marred by forks that were soft for hard riding, but the practical, well-finished and reliable RS made a very capable long-haul machine. Its success did much to help restore BMW's fortunes.

BMW K100RS (1984)	
Engine	Liquid-cooled dohc eight-valve horizontal four
Capacity	987cc (67 x 70mm)
Maximum power	90bhp @ 7300rpm
Transmission	Five-speed, shaft final drive
Frame	Tubular steel
Suspension	Telescopic front; single shock rear
Brakes	Twin discs front; disc rear
Weight	556lb (253kg) wet
Top speed	135mph (217km/h)

Below: The RS added a stylish and aerodynamically efficient half fairing to the standard K100's format of 987cc four-cylinder engine, horizontal cylinders and shaft final drive.

Yamaha RD500LC

Yamaha did not hold back when, following many requests, the firm finally developed a roadgoing version of its all-conquering 500cc V4 Grand Prix bike. The RD500LC was launched in 1984, as Californian Eddie Lawson was riding Yamaha's factory OW76 to the World Championship. It was a stunning replica with a 499cc liquid-cooled two-stroke V4 powerplant, a light and well-equipped chassis, and a full fairing whose red and white paint scheme added to the GP image.

The 90bhp V4 engine was essentially a pair of RD250LC engines with cylinders set at 50 degrees, and bottom ends geared together. It shared details including bore and stroke dimensions and exhaust power valves with the race motor. The RD500LC had a frame of square-section steel tubes, though the otherwise near-identical Japanese market RZV500R followed the racebike by having an aluminium frame. Both roadster variants featured anti-dive equipped forks and a horizontal monoshock beneath the engine.

Engine performance was uniquely thrilling, with a flat feeling at low revs before the two-stroke came alive at 6000rpm with a crackling exhaust wail and a fearsome burst of acceleration towards its top speed of almost 140mph (225km/h). Handling, braking and roadholding were outstanding, thanks to the high-quality chassis and weight of just 392lb (198kg). Unfortunately for Yamaha, pre-launch excitement did not translate into sales success. That was partly due to the V4's high price, vibration and heavy fuel consumption. And partly because for roadgoing use it was simply too single-minded and racy – too much of a genuine GP replica.

Honda VF1000R

The VF1000R was launched in 1984 as an exotic flagship for Honda's V4 range, which grew in that year to include six models from 400 to 1000cc. With its tuned 998cc motor, high-tech chassis and full fairing in Honda's red, white and blue colours, the VF was designed as an all-conquering street-legal racebike in the style of its straight-four predecessor the CB1100R.

Its liquid-cooled, 16-valve motor was an uprated version of the 90-degree V4 from the VF1000F, a half-faired streetbike that was launched simultaneously. Gear-driven camshafts were among the modifications that boosted peak output by 6bhp to 122bhp, making the 1000R Honda's most powerful streetbike yet. Its chassis specification was equally upmarket, combining a frame of square-section steel tubes with air-assisted forks, TRAC anti-dive, Pro-Link monoshock, and four-piston front brake calipers. Despite having a carbon-fibre reinforced fairing the 1000R weighed a substantial 524lb (238kg).

The big V4 was a wonderful road bike, even so. Its engine churned out smooth power throughout the range, giving effortlessly smooth high-speed cruising plus warp-speed acceleration to a maximum of 150mph (241km/h). The sporty but roomy riding position and excellent fairing helped make the Honda as comfortable as it was fast, and its high-speed stability was immense. But its weight and conservative steering geometry combined to make the VF a handful at slower speeds, severely limiting its racing potential. The lack of track glory combined with a high price to keep demand for the VF1000R far below the level Honda had expected.

Above: The VF1000R was too long and heavy to be as successful a production racer as Honda had hoped, but it still handled very well.

Below: The Honda's full fairing contributed to its impressive top speed and helped make the big V4 a comfortable long-distance roadster.

Kawasaki GPZ900R

T
he GPZ900R heralded a new era of superbike design when it stormed onto the roads in 1984. With its sleek full fairing, compact build and liquid-cooled, 16-valve engine, the Ninja was very different to the previous breed of big, air cooled, two-valves-per-cylinder fours that suddenly looked old-fashioned. The GPZ was a 908cc bike that felt like a 750 – and had the performance to outclass its 1100cc rivals.

Kawasaki's new engine incorporated a balancer shaft, cam chain at the end of the crank, and alternator above the six-speed gearbox. It was small, light and powerful, though its 113bhp peak was slightly below that of the firm's air-cooled GPz1100. The frame used the engine as a stressed member, combining steel main tubes with an alloy rear subframe. The forks incorporated anti-dive; rear suspension was a Uni-Trak monoshock with air-assistance and adjustable rebound damping. The sharply styled fairing kept most of the wind off the rider, who leant forward to near-flat bars.

Performance was a breathtaking blend of speed and refinement. The Ninja was docile and controllable at slow speed, respectably light, and most of all fast. Top speed was over 150mph (241km/h), with searing acceleration at high revs. The rigid frame, firm suspension and 16-inch front wheel gave stability with light, precise steering. Brakes were superbly powerful. The Kawasaki was also practical, combining a generous fuel range with details including luggage hooks and a grab-rail. It became hugely popular and remained little changed until 1990, when chassis updates gave it a new role as a budget sports-tourer.

Above: *The GPZ900R's sharply styled full fairing helped make it faster than many naked superbikes with bigger, more powerful engines.*

Below: *The Ninja's 908cc liquid-cooled, 16-valve engine heralded a new generation of powerful and sophisticated Kawasaki fours.*

Harley-Davidson FXST Softail

The Softail, with its new-generation Evolution V-twin engine and a classical 'hardtail' look due to hidden rear shock units, was one of the key models with which Harley-Davidson launched its dramatic revival in the mid-1980s. The comeback had begun in 1981, when the company was bought from AMF (American Machine and Foundry) by a group of senior managers. Three years later Harley introduced five models, including the new Softail, powered by a 1340cc powerplant that was superior in every way to the old Shovelhead V-twin.

Harley's new owners knew that reliability and quality control must improve dramatically if the Milwaukee marque was to compete with the Japanese manufacturers whose products had outclassed and outsold its bikes in the 1970s. A huge effort was made to ensure that the new Evolution motor, which retained the traditional air-cooled, 45-degree, pushrod-operated layout, was good enough. It produced 55bhp with a broad spread of torque, and proved lighter, cooler-running, more efficient and far more reliable than its predecessor.

The Evo unit was particularly at home in the new Softail, whose classic look, enhanced by its apparently unsuspended rear end, combined with the new engine's improved performance and durability to make the model popular. Harley reacted quickly, and two years later introduced the more retro-styled Heritage Softail plus the Softail Custom, featuring a disc rear wheel. Such was the success of these and the other Evolution models that by 1987 Harley was listed on the New York Stock Exchange, and well on the way to recovery.

Harley-Davidson FXST Softail (1984)	
Engine	Air-cooled ohv pushrod four-valve 45-degree V-twin
Capacity	1338cc (89 x 108mm)
Maximum power	55bhp @ 5500rpm
Transmission	Four-speed, chain final drive
Frame	Tubular steel
Suspension	Telescopic front; twin shocks rear
Brakes	Single disc front & rear
Weight	628lb (285kg)
Top speed	110mph (177km/h)

Below: The Softail housed Harley's sweet-running new Evolution V-twin engine in a hardtail-look chassis with hidden rear shocks, creating a bike with an appealing blend of refined performance and traditional style.

Yamaha V-Max

It is a remarkable achievement for a manufacturer to produce a model that will remain in its line-up for more than two decades with its look and performance almost unchanged, especially when that performance is central to the bike's appeal. That's what Yamaha managed with the V-Max, whose unique blend of street-rod styling, muscular V4 powerplant and marginal chassis created one of motorcycling's longest-running success stories.

The V-Max was designed in the US and launched in 1985. It made an immediate impact due largely to an 1198cc, dohc, 16-valve engine whose 143bhp output made it by far the world's most powerful streetbike. Yamaha had tuned the 72-degree, liquid-cooled V4 of its Venture tourer with hot cams, high compression and big valves, then added V-boost, a system that linked the carburettors to give extra high-rev power. The bike's appeal was enhanced by its dramatic, cut-down styling, highlighted by fake air scoops jutting from either side of the dummy fuel tank.

Straight-line performance was shoulder-splittingly strong. The V-Max catapulted away from a standstill leaving a black stripe on the road with its spinning back tyre, the fattest yet seen. More streamlined bikes could top the Yamaha's 140mph (225km/h) top speed, but nothing left the line or generated adrenaline quite like the V-Max. And although the near-600lb (273kg) bike's simple twin-shock chassis gave handling that was distinctly unstable at times, that merely added to its appeal. The V-Max's wild image helped it remain popular, with few updates, well into the 21st century.

Above and below: The stunningly squat and muscular V-Max look was barely modified through more than two decades of production, although ironically the Yamaha was initially detuned for many markets where its mighty 1198cc V4 engine was regarded as too powerful.

Suzuki GSX-R750

Suzuki's stunningly fast and light GSX-R750 ripped up the superbike rulebook in 1985 with a blend of race-derived design, scorching performance and uncompromising character. The GSX-R was the first true Japanese race replica; a faithful roadgoing version of Suzuki's 1000cc factory endurance machine. Its instant and lasting success inspired rival manufacturers to follow, creating the super-sports category of track-bred machines.

Race-replica bikes dated back to the 1920s and beyond, as firms including Scott, Rudge and Velocette had sold bikes based on the previous year's TT-winning machines. But the modern era had seen nothing like the GSX-R750, whose endurance-racer style twin-headlamp fairing gave a look very similar to that of the factory bike – and whose innovative, oil-cooled four-cylinder engine was held by a remarkably light and effective aluminium-framed chassis.

The 749cc engine followed its GSX750 predecessor in its dohc, 16-valve layout, but almost every component was redesigned for more power or reduced size and weight. The GSX-R employed a novel (for bikes) system of oil-cooling that dispensed with the bulk of a water jacket. Suzuki's development team, led by former race

Below: The GSX-R's styling and its format of twin-headlamp full fairing, aluminium frame and 18-inch wheels came directly from Suzuki's works endurance racebikes.

Above: Suzuki's powerful dohc, 16-valve engine was innovative in its use of oil cooling and its emphasis on weight reduction in every area.

Above left: The GSX-R's light weight and good aerodynamics were as important as its 100bhp power output in generating the bike's stunning straight-line speed.

team manager Etsuo Yokouchi, also saved weight by using magnesium instead of aluminium for the cam cover. Peak power was a highly competitive 100bhp.

Suzuki's ground-breaking use of aluminium resulted in a frame that combined cast-aluminium sections with extruded main tubes, and whose weight of 18lb (8kg) was half that of the GSX750's less rigid steel frame. Front forks were thick 41mm units, reinforced by an aluminium brace; a damping-adjustable monoshock supported the rear. At 388lb (176kg) the GSX-R was far lighter than many middleweights, let alone any 750cc rival.

There was no mistaking its uniquely aggressive intent, confirmed by low, clip-on bars and a foam-mounted instrument console whose speedometer was easily removed for racing. The bike's performance very much lived up to its image. The Suzuki was rideable at low revs but its delivery was flat until 7000rpm, when the motor suddenly came alive, howling through its four-into-one pipe as the bike surged smoothly towards a maximum of 145mph (233km/h).

The GSX-R's firm, well-controlled suspension and powerful twin-disc front brake gave it an advantage over every other bike in cornering and stopping. All was not perfect, and the original model's occasional high-speed wobble prompted Suzuki to introduce a slightly longer swing-arm in 1986. As a roadster the GSX-R was far from practical or comfortable, though its reasonably broad seat and strong pillion grab-rail were partial compensation for its narrow mirrors, high pegs and poor fuel range.

Few GSX-R750 riders were concerned about such details. The Suzuki was built for speed and it delivered, earning a cult following and inspiring a family of GSX-R fours in sizes from 250 to 1100cc. It was repeatedly updated over the next two decades, eventually gaining a liquid-cooled engine and an aluminium beam frame like many of its super-sports rivals – and throughout it all retaining the race-bred performance and aggressive image of the original, incomparable GSX-R750.

Suzuki GSX-R750 (1985)	
Engine Oil-cooled dohc 16-valve four	
Capacity 749cc (70 x 48.7mm)	
Maximum power 100bhp @ 10,500rpm	
Transmission Six-speed, chain final drive	
Frame Aluminium twin downtube	
Suspension Telescopic front; single shock rear	
Brakes Twin discs front; disc rear	
Weight 388lb (176kg) dry	
Top speed 145mph (233km/h)	

Yamaha FZ750

The powerful and versatile FZ750 was not an outstanding sales success following its introduction in 1985, but it will long be remembered for pioneering the angled-forward, 20-valve engine layout on which Yamaha's four-cylinder sports bikes would be based for the next two decades and more. The firm had struggled to create a four-stroke superbike to match the popularity of its smaller two-strokes, and the FZ750 was an imaginative attempt.

Its five-valves-per-cylinder layout (three inlets, two exhaust), fed by downdraft carburettors, was claimed to give more efficient breathing than conventional four-valve designs, and the 749cc FZ unit was an impressive performer. Its 105bhp maximum was backed up by generous torque through the range, and the motor also proved outstandingly economical and robust. Chassis design was relatively conservative, based around a rectangular-section steel frame. Air-assisted forks held a 16-inch front wheel; rear suspension was by vertical monoshock.

The FZ couldn't match the glamour or outright speed of Suzuki's GSX-R750, launched at the same time, but it was a superb all-rounder. Its smooth, flexible engine kicked harder at high revs to send the FZ howling to a top speed of over 140mph (225km/h). The fairly upright riding position allowed comfortable cruising, although the half fairing's screen was slightly low. Handling was precise yet stable, the chassis let down only by a front brake that lacked initial bite. Disappointing sales improved only slightly a year later, when the FZ gained a full fairing. But the 20-valve four had made a vital contribution to Yamaha's superbike story.

Yamaha FZ750 (1985)	
Engine	Liquid-cooled, dohc 20-valve transverse four
Capacity	749cc (68 x 51.6mm)
Maximum power	105bhp @ 10,500rpm
Transmission	Six-speed, chain final drive
Frame	Steel twin downtube
Suspension	Telescopic front; monoshock rear
Brakes	Twin discs front; disc rear
Weight	460lb (209kg)
Top speed	145mph (233km/h)

Below: The original FZ750 featured a half fairing that displayed its innovative 749cc four-cylinder engine, with its angled-forward cylinders and 20-valve top end.

Bimota DB1

As Bimota's first ever Ducati-powered model and first all-Italian machine, the DB1 was an important milestone in the Rimini firm's history. And the significance of the 750cc V-twin with the curvaceous, all-enveloping bodywork goes much further than that, for it was the DB1's unexpected sales success, following its launch in 1986, that rescued Bimota from one of the most serious of the marque's numerous periods of financial difficulty.

Much of the DB1's appeal was due to its unmistakable appearance. Chief engineer Federico Martini's innovative fairing/tank/seat unit enclosed the whole bike in a streamlined glass-fibre shell that gave the diminutive Bimota a very different look to the Ducati F1 from which its engine was derived. The sohc, 90-degree desmo V-twin produced 76bhp and acted as a stressed member of a tubular-steel ladder frame that could have been built by Ducati itself. Marzocchi suspension, Brembo brakes and wide 16-inch wheels wearing low-profile Pirelli rubber completed an exotic specification.

By superbike standards the little Bimota was not particularly fast, though its crisp carburation and strong midrange gave vivid acceleration as the free-breathing V-twin roared towards its 130mph (209km/h) top speed. The DB1's light weight of just 354lb (161kg) also boosted its straight-line performance, as well as providing superbly agile handling in conjunction with the rigid frame and firm suspension. Braking and roadholding were also exemplary, but it was the DB1's blend of unique style, V-twin character and relatively competitive price that did most to make it a vitally important success for Bimota.

Above: *The DB1 was not particularly powerful, but its streamlined bodywork helped give respectable straight-line performance to complement the Bimota's wonderfully agile handling.*

Above: *The Bimota's unique cockpit view included a machined aluminium top yoke, plus Marzocchi fork tops which incorporated the hydraulic master cylinders for the clutch and front brake.*

Honda VFR750F

T he VFR750F was arguably the most important bike that Honda has ever built, as well as one of the best. It was introduced in 1986 by a manufacturer desperate to restore a reputation for high-quality engineering that had been badly shaken by a series of unimpressive models, culminating in the disastrously unreliable VF750F of three years earlier. The VFR750F, launched into a hugely competitive 750cc market, had to be both good and reliable. Fortunately for Honda, it was.

Its 748cc engine retained the VF's 90-degree, 16-valve, liquid-cooled V4 format but had cam drive by gears instead of chains. Lighter valves, pistons and conrods helped boost peak output by 15bhp to 105bhp. A light and rigid new aluminium frame contributed to a competitive weight figure of 436lb (198kg). Air-assisted forks held a 16-inch front wheel; the single shock benefited from a remote pre-load adjuster. Riding position was roomy, and the fairing was finished in dark blue or white to highlight the bike's all-rounder status.

The VFR thoroughly deserved the description. It was quick, with a top speed of around 150mph (241km/h). More importantly, its strong midrange response and smooth, free-flowing power delivery gave a wonderfully relaxed ride. Handling was exemplary, combining easy steering with reassuring stability. Suspension was slightly soft for hard riding but the efficient fairing helped make the Honda comfortable over long distances. Most importantly of all, its engine was impeccably reliable. Before long the VFR750F was regarded as the ultimate sports-tourer, and Honda's problems were a distant memory.

Above: The VFR's styling was relatively restrained, but Honda had succeeded in giving the V4 outstanding performance and refinement.

Above: Excellent handling combined with the VFR's speed, comfort and reliability to make the V4 a big success and restore Honda's reputation for high-quality engineering.

Suzuki GSX-R1100

Having rocked the superbike world with the GSX-R750 in 1985, Suzuki produced a less imaginative but even faster and more rounded follow-up a year later in the very similar shape of the GSX-R1100. As well as sharing the smaller model's endurance racer inspired twin-headlamp styling, the 1100 followed its format of oil-cooled, 16-valve engine and aluminium-framed chassis. The new bike's 1052cc motor was not only considerably more powerful, with a maximum of 125bhp, it was also notably more flexible and robust.

The GSX-R1100's frame, welded from cast and extruded aluminium sections, was a stronger version of the 750's radically light structure, and incorporated a steering damper. Identical, anti-dive equipped front forks combined with a new rear shock, wider 18-inch wheels and tyres, and bigger front brake discs. At 433lb (197kg) dry the GSX-R1100 was 45lb (20kg) heavier than its smaller sibling but remarkably light for an open-class bike.

Predictably the GSX-R1100's broad spread of power, light weight and high quality chassis made for a magnificent sports machine. The Suzuki streaked to a top speed of 155mph (249km/h) at an unprecedented rate, and provided fierce acceleration at almost any engine speed. Its brakes were powerful, and it combined precise handling with improved stability over the 750. Inevitably the racy GSX-R was not ideal for town or two-up riding, but its leant-forward riding position, tall screen and broad seat even made it respectably comfortable for high-speed blasts. And for pure performance on road or track, no other production bike even came close.

Above: The GSX-R1100's styling followed that of the 750, but the bigger machine had a stronger aluminium frame as well as the extra cylinder capacity that gave superbly flexible power delivery.

Suzuki GSX-R1100 (1986)

Engine Oil-cooled dohc 16-valve transverse four

Capacity 1052cc (76 x 58mm)

Maximum power 125bhp @ 8500rpm

Transmission Five-speed, chain final drive

Frame Aluminium twin downtube

Suspension Telescopic front; single shock rear

Brakes Twin discs front; disc rear

Weight 433lb (197kg)

Top speed 155mph (249km/h)

Yamaha FJ1200

It was ironic that Yamaha's first successful four-stroke superbike, after years of disappointment, became the outstanding machine in its class almost by accident. The FJ1100, launched in 1984, had been billed by Yamaha as an 'out-and-out high performance sports machine', but had been recast as a sports-tourer after being outgunned by Kawasaki's GPZ900R. Two years later Yamaha enlarged the FJ's air-cooled, 16-valve engine to 1188cc, creating the FJ1200 that became a sports-touring legend during a decade of production.

The extra capacity added further to the wonderfully flexible power delivery that had arguably been the FJ1100's biggest asset. The bigger model's peak output of 125bhp was unchanged, as was its top speed of about 150mph (241km/h). But throughout much of the rev range the FJ1200 motor produced even more of the smooth torque that allowed effortless high-speed travel, often making the five-speed gearbox almost redundant. Although the FJ was heavy, at 576lb (261kg), and its suspension was slightly soft for hard riding, the big four handled well and was impressively manoeuvrable.

Comfort and practicality were other attributes that made the FJ well suited to a sports-touring role. Final drive was by chain rather than shaft, but the Yamaha's half fairing and tall screen combined with features including a large fuel tank, roomy riding position and broad dual seat to make it fine long-haul machine. Over the years it was upgraded with a 17-inch front wheel, uprated suspension and ABS brakes. Its style, character and reputation as an outstanding sports-tourer remained very much intact.

Above: The FJ1200 closely followed the look of the original 1100cc model. The Yamaha's long-distance potential was often enhanced by panniers.

Below: Although the FJ lacked the agility and ground clearance of the fastest sports bikes, it went round corners well enough to provide plenty of entertainment.

Honda CBR600F

There was a good reason why Honda's CBR600F was the world's best-selling motorcycle in the late 1980s. The CBR was not the most technically advanced or exciting bike the firm had ever built, but the four-cylinder middleweight provided a combination of performance, versatility, reliability and value for money that no other bike could match. The introduction of both the 600F and the similarly styled CBR1000F, which was also launched in 1987, represented a change of emphasis for Honda, back from V4s to a straight-four engine layout.

Not that the CBRs made a big feature of their liquid-cooled, dohc 16-valve powerplants, which were hidden behind rounded bodywork that provided efficient aerodynamics and reduced the expense that had to be spent on their presentation. The smaller model's 599cc engine was similar in layout to that of Kawasaki's GPZ600R, which had been launched two years earlier, and produced more power to a maximum of 85bhp. The Honda's chassis was down-to-earth, comprising a steel frame, conventional telescopic forks, Pro-Link monoshock and triple discs.

The CBR's format might not have been exceptional, but its performance certainly was – at least by middleweight standards. The refined and well-built Honda required plenty of revs for rapid acceleration, but cruised smoothly and gave plenty of entertainment as it surged to its 140mph (225km/h) top speed. Excellent handling and braking combined with the four's reasonable comfort and competitive price to make an outstanding all-rounder. The CBR600F's global popularity fully vindicated Honda's return to the straight four.

Above: The CBR's all-enveloping bodywork gave good aerodynamics and kept its 599cc liquid-cooled, 16-valve engine hidden from view.

Below: Fine handling was among the attributes that helped make the fast and competitively priced CBR600F one of the most successful bikes of recent decades.

Norton Classic

The launch of the rotary-engined Classic in 1987 confirmed the start of a new era for Norton. The famous British marque, by now a small company making spare parts, had begun development of a rotary machine in the mid-'70s, and had revised it through 13 years of low-budget development, with the help of several UK police forces. Finally the Classic was ready, powered by a 588cc, air-cooled, twin-chamber rotary unit whose 79bhp output matched that of Honda's CBR600F.

Norton's painstaking development had been worthwhile, because the Classic was a capable and enjoyable machine. The rotary motor was hesitant at low revs but strong through the midrange and supremely smooth, giving a pleasant high-speed cruising feel and a top speed of about 135mph (217km/h). Poor fuel consumption and a rather crude five-speed gearbox were less welcome features. The unfaired Classic was stable at speed, and handled well despite a dated chassis layout comprising a pressed-steel spine frame, gaitered front forks and twin shocks.

Paintwork in Norton's traditional silver gave nostalgic appeal, and the practical Classic incorporated a comfortable dual seat and enclosed drive chain. The limited run of 100 bikes quickly sold, despite a high price. Norton developed a touring version, the Commander, and hit the headlines when workers used a tuned, 135bhp rotary motor as the basis for a stunning racebike that Steve Spray rode to two National Championships in 1989. The stylish F1 roadgoing replica followed, but problems and a high price resulted in Norton's revival fading in the mid-'90s.

Above: Norton's 588cc rotary engine had twin chambers and was cooled by air with the help of comprehensive finning.

Below: The Classic handled well despite a twin-shock chassis that was old-fashioned by the time of its launch in 1987.

Harley-Davidson XLH1200 Sportster

Above: High bars and tiny tank were part of the Sportster's appeal, for its riders as well as for everyone else.

Left: Lean and simple styling, a big V-twin engine and a keen price helped make the Sportster hugely popular.

More than three decades after the introduction of Harley-Davidson's Sportster in 1957, the XLH1200 Sportster showed that the original blend of lean V-twin style still had much to offer. The Sportster had gone through many changes since that first model, notably in 1972 when its engine was enlarged to 1000cc, and in 1986 when the first Evolution-engined Sportster was launched with the old 883cc capacity. Harley soon added an 1100cc version, and in 1988 bored out its motor to 1202cc to create the XLH1200.

The classical Sportster look of high bars, tiny gas tank and big air-cooled V-twin engine was unchanged, but the new bike was a distinct improvement. Its reshaped combustion chambers combined with the extra capacity to increase peak output to 60bhp. A new carburettor improved low-rev response and helped make the Sportster enjoyably quick away from the line. It cruised with a pleasant V-twin feel, although the solid-mounted motor's vibration meant this was best done well below the 115mph (185km/h) top speed.

Handling was stable, helped by thicker fork tubes, and the Evolution V-twin motor proved reliable. The Sportster's style, performance and competitive price made it a hit. The smaller 883 version was also popular, boosted by Harley innovations including the Hugger, with its extra-low seat, and an offer to buy the bike back at cost price if the owner upgraded. By the time Harley gave the XLH1200 a five-speed gearbox and belt final drive, the Sportster had become the best-selling bike in the US.

Harley-Davidson XLH1200 Sportster (1988)

Engine	Air-cooled ohv pushrod four-valve 45-degree V-twin
Capacity	1202cc (85 x 89mm)
Maximum power	60bhp @ 5000rpm
Transmission	Four-speed, chain final drive
Frame	Tubular steel
Suspension	Telescopic front; twin shocks rear
Brakes	Single disc front & rear
Weight	492lb (223kg)
Top speed	115mph (185km/h)

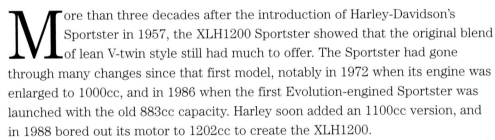

Honda RC30

The exotic RC30 that Honda unleashed in 1988 was far more than another race replica. It was remarkably close to being a street-legal version of the factory RVF750 that had dominated Formula One and endurance racing in recent seasons. Produced in relatively small numbers and bristling with high-quality components, the 749cc V4 was the most single-minded and outrageously capable roadster Honda had ever created.

Even the most authentic of previous race replicas could not compare with the RC30, which was conceived as a money-no-object basis for competition success. Officially known as the VFR750R, it followed the factory RVF to an unprecedented degree. Its compact twin-headlamp fairing and single seat unit, lightweight twin-spar aluminium frame and single-sided swing arm gave a look almost identical to that of the all-conquering works racer.

Honda's single-sided Pro-Arm had been pioneered on the innovative Elf racebikes before being fitted to the RVF endurance machines to save time on tyre-changes. Most engineers dismissed Honda's claim that it was stiffer than

Below: The RC30 looked almost identical to the all-conquering factory RVF endurance racer, from its compact twin-headlamp fairing to the single seat and apparently unsuspended rear wheel, held by a single-sided swing-arm.

conventional swing-arms of the same weight, but the view of the RC30's apparently unsuspended rear wheel added to its appeal – and helped justify a price almost double that of Honda's VFR750F roadster.

The liquid-cooled, 90-degree V4 was a tuned and lightened version of the 750F's dohc, 16-valve unit. Peak output was 112bhp, an increase of 7bhp. The RC30 used a 360-degree crankshaft, like the RVF racers but unlike the 180-degree 750F, as this improved drive out of corners. Con rods were forged from titanium. Larger carbs, twin curved radiators and a complex single-pipe exhaust system were further RFV features.

Straight-line performance was gloriously strong, enhanced by an abundance of smooth, free-revving power from low revs. Like its factory racebike relation, the V4 accelerated in a deceptively effortless way, with a flat exhaust drone. The close-ratio gearbox's ultra-tall first ratio, good for over 80mph (130km/h), was inconvenient in town but helped keep the RC30 revving hard as it stormed towards its 155mph (250km/h) top speed.

The Honda's racetrack heritage was reflected in its ergonomics and detailing. The screen and handlebars were low; footrests high. The rev-counter and temperature gauge were foam-mounted; the speedo was separate for easy removal. The compact wheelbase and steering geometry matched the RVF's, and at 407lb (185kg) the RC30 was light by roadgoing standards.

Premium-quality cycle parts included 43mm forks and 310mm diameter front brake discs, like those of the RVF. Front and rear suspension were adjustable for compression and rebound damping, and helped give a taut and well-balanced cornering feel. The bike's breathtaking agility and braking power were complimented by impressive stability.

Honda had created the RC30 to win races, and it did not disappoint. Californian ace Fred Merkel rode a race-kitted RC30 to consecutive Superbike world titles in 1988 and '89, a feat matched by Britain's Carl Fogarty in the Formula One class. The RC30 won many other titles, too, but it's for its brilliance as a streetbike that the ultimate V4 race-replica will be most fondly remembered.

Honda RC30 (1988)	
Engine	Liquid-cooled dohc 16-valve 90-degree V4
Capacity	748cc (70 x 48.6mm)
Maximum power	112bhp @ 11,000rpm
Transmission	Six-speed, chain final drive
Frame	Aluminium twin spar
Suspension	Telescopic front; single shock rear
Brakes	Twin discs front; disc rear
Weight	407lb (185kg) dry
Top speed	155mph (250km/h)

Below left: Components including the rigid twin-spar aluminium frame were ready for racing with no modification, unlike the RC30's relatively heavy and restrictive standard exhaust system.

Below: The Honda's chassis rigidity, racy geometry and high-quality suspension parts combined to give superb handling, though the RC30 required careful setting-up to give of its best.

Bimota YB8

By the late 1980s the Japanese manufacturers had dramatically improved the quality of their top superbikes' chassis, but there was still scope for a small firm to create something extra special around a powerful four-cylinder engine. That was most emphatically illustrated by Bimota's YB8, whose format of aluminium beam-framed chassis and four-cylinder Yamaha powerplant followed that of the small Italian firm's 750cc YB4, which had won the Formula One World Championship in 1987.

Bimota had quickly followed its Italian factory rider Virginio Ferrari's triumph by releasing a stylish roadgoing replica, the YB4ie, that housed an FZ750 engine in a chassis almost identical to that of the racebike. The YB4ie was soon joined in Bimota's range by a similar YB6 model, powered by the 20-valve engine from Yamaha's FZR1000. When Yamaha revamped its motor and added an exhaust power valve to create the FZR1000 EXUP, Bimota adopted that unit for its own updated model, called the YB6 EXUP or, more commonly, the YB8.

The combination of Yamaha's powerful, unburstable engine and Bimota's light, lavishly equipped chassis made the YB8 arguably the ultimate super-sports bike of its day. Its free-breathing exhaust system helped the 1002cc motor produce a claimed 147bhp, with gloriously strong midrange acceleration. At just 407lb (185kg) the Bimota was 50lb (23kg) lighter than the mass-produced Yamaha, and its ultra-rigid frame, firm Marzocchi suspension and Brembo brakes gave sublime handling and stopping power. Inevitably the hand-built YB8's price was high, but it became one of Bimota's most successful-ever models.

Above: The huge, light and stiff aluminium twin-spar frame combined with the Bimota's high-class suspension parts to give brilliant handling.

Above left: The fully faired YB8's excellent aerodynamics added to the straight-line performance provided by the powerful 1002cc, 20-valve motor from Yamaha's FZR1000.

Bimota YB8 (1989)

Engine Liquid-cooled, dohc 20-valve transverse four

Capacity 1002cc (75.5 x 56mm)

Maximum power 147bhp @ 10,000rpm

Transmission Six-speed, chain final drive

Frame Aluminium twin spar

Suspension Telescopic front; monoshock rear

Brakes Twin discs front; disc rear

Weight 407lb (185kg) wet

Top speed 170mph (274km/h)

Buell RS1200

Buell Motorcycles' production of innovative, Harley-Davidson powered streetbikes dates back to 1989 and the introduction of the RS1200. Erik Buell was a former racer and Harley engineer who had set up his own firm in a Wisconsin barn, and had used his old employer's V-twin engine to power an ingenious, fully faired racebike called the RR1000. Buell's next step was to create a roadster, the RS1200, whose half fairing highlighted the Harley connection by leaving its Sportster 1200 engine on display.

The RS1200's cut-down bodywork also revealed its high-quality chassis. The tubular-steel trellis frame held the engine via Buell's ingenious Uniplanar rubber-mounting system. Forks were Marzocchi units modified with Buell's own anti-dive system. The rear shock sat horizontally below the engine, and worked in tension rather than compression. Even the wheels and four-piston front brake calipers were Buell's work. So was the striking glass-fibre bodywork, which incorporated a seat hump that hinged to become a pillion back-rest.

Boosted by a SuperTrapp exhaust, the pushrod-operated V-twin motor produced 70bhp. It gave the RS1200 – also known as the Westwind – lively acceleration to a top speed of 120mph (193km/h), with strong low-rev response and greatly reduced vibration. The RS1200's short wheelbase, racy geometry and weight of 450lb (250kg) provided light and precise handling, too. Inevitably the Buell was expensive, costing twice as much as a standard Sportster. But it was a success, and began a line of imaginative Buell streetbikes that was expanded after Harley took over the company in the 1990s.

Above and below: The Buell's half faring left its Harley V-twin powerplant on display. It also revealed the innovative chassis with its tubular-steel frame, partial rubber-mounting system and under-slung rear shock absorber, located below the engine alongside the exhaust muffler.

BMW K1

The K1 sportster's bright, all-enveloping bodywork made it a dramatic looking machine by any standards, let alone those of traditionally conservative BMW. The German marque had decided its image needed updating, and the K1 was the result. Its ultra-slippery shape was prompted by BMW's decision to build a four-cylinder sportster governed by Germany's 100bhp power limit. When giving away 20bhp to rival superbikes in export markets, a low drag coefficient was vital.

Behind the bodywork was a tuned, 16-valve version of the K100's 987cc four-cylinder engine, featuring horizontal, liquid-cooled cylinders. A new engine-management system and increased compression boosted power by ten per cent to exactly 100bhp. The K100-based steel frame held Marzocchi forks and Brembo brakes, with optional ABS. The rear shock benefited from Paralever, BMW's system of rods that reduced the drive shaft's traditional adverse effect on handling.

For covering long distances at speed the K1 was impressive, helped by its efficient fairing, comfortable riding position and excellent fuel economy. Its engine combined a broad spread of torque with enough top-end power for a top speed approaching 150mph (241km/h). And although the BMW was long and heavy at 468lb (284kg), it had stable handling, taut suspension and powerful brakes. The K1 lacked the speed and agility of a true sportster, and for touring was marred by its frustrating inability to carry a pillion and luggage simultaneously. But the K1 was fast and capable, and succeeded in giving BMW's image a valuable boost.

Above: The K1's large front mudguard was an integral element of its aerodynamic bodywork, helping to direct air around the bike.

Below: BMW's emphasis on a low drag coefficient resulted in a striking superbike that was very fast given its modest 100bhp maximum output.

Kawasaki ZXR750

Kawasaki's ZXR750 showed that style was as important as technology when designing a race-replica sports bike, and that a low price could be as valuable as high performance. The liquid-cooled four incorporated little innovative engineering, and its 105bhp power output was as unexceptional as its dry weight figure of 452lb (205kg). But the Kawasaki's sleek lines, striking paintwork and ostentatious air ducts gave it an appeal that was enhanced by a competitive price.

Its motor was a tuned version of the dohc, 16-valve unit from Kawasaki's GPX750, and featured bigger valves, a higher compression ratio and a lightened crankshaft although its output was barely increased. The ZXR's aluminium beam frame was very rigid but not particularly light, as the bike was slightly heavier than the steel-framed GPX. Big front brake discs and fat radial rubber added to the aggressive image provided by the air ducts that swept back from the nose of its twin-headlamp fairing.

The Kawasaki provided more than enough performance to be fun. Its engine was rev-happy, smooth and powerful enough for a top speed of 150mph (241km/h). The racy riding position was ideal for control at speed, and the brakes were powerful. Handling was precise and stable, though not exactly agile, and compromised by the harsh rear shock. Overall the Kawasaki was not the fastest of the super-sports 750s in 1989, nor was it the lightest or most sophisticated. But for style and value for money it was unbeatable – and, as its popularity confirmed, that meant a lot.

Above: Large twin ducts fed the 16-valve motor with air from the front of the fairing, and more importantly, added to the Kawasaki's aggressive, race-developed image.

Ducati 851

The 851 was the bike with which Ducati embraced the modern age of liquid cooling and four-valves-per-cylinder technology – and came out fighting with a fast and charismatic contender. The 851cc V-twin, which retained the Bologna marque's traditional 90-degree cylinder angle, was designed by young chief engineer Massimo Bordi. His predecessor Fabio Taglioni had always rejected thoughts of an eight-valve V-twin, but Bordi pressed ahead with an engine that also employed fuel-injection instead of carburettors.

Bordi's dohc, eight-valve V-twin adapted Ducati's familiar desmodromic method of positive valve closure to give improved cylinder breathing. The result was extra midrange output and a maximum of 100bhp that made the 851 the most powerful production Ducati yet. The motor formed a stressed member of a typical tubular-

Below: The revised, 1989-model 851 handled superbly thanks to a combination of stiff frame, excellent suspension and steering geometry that suited its new 17-inch wheels.

steel ladder frame, which held Marzocchi suspension and Brembo brakes. The bike's rounded full fairing and single seat were finished in a patriotic red, white and green paint scheme.

The original 851 made a huge splash on its launch in 1988 – and received a distinctly mixed reception. Its engine was a triumph: powerful, smooth and refined, it provided thrilling top-end acceleration plus plenty of midrange torque. But the chassis was flawed. Problems of supply resulted in early 851s being fitted with 16-inch wheels, instead of the 17-inchers it had been designed for. The result was unpredictable handling, and some very confused owners.

The following year, Ducati introduced a comprehensively overhauled V-twin, finished in Italian racing red, to make the 851 the bike it should have been all along. Its engine was uprated with a modified injection system, new cams, higher compression ratio and reworked exhaust, increasing peak output to 104bhp. The frame was modified, the rear shock replaced, and most importantly the Ducati was fitted with the 17-inch wheels it had been designed to wear.

The result was a transformed bike with handsome looks, breathtaking performance, an addictive V-twin character – and handling to Ducati's traditional high standard. The sophisticated eight-valve powerplant generated vast reserves of torque from low revs to 10,000rpm. Tweaking the throttle sent the 851 thundering at a fearsome rate towards a top speed approaching 150mph (241km/h).

Better still, its taut and well-equipped chassis was now an ideal match for the engine. At 396lb (180kg) the Ducati was light, and its blend of rigid frame, high-quality suspension and now finely tuned geometry resulted in agile handling plus confidence-inspiring stability. Roadholding and ground clearance were first class, the latter enhanced by a slimmer fairing. Larger Brembo front brake discs gave even more powerful stopping.

In many markets the 851 was also reduced in price, which further enhanced its popularity, although it was still far from cheap. As well as being an outstanding roadster, it formed the basis of the snarling factory racebikes that took Raymond Roche and Doug Polen to three consecutive World Superbike titles. The eight-valve V-twin engine was then enlarged to power the restyled 916 that continued Ducati's success story through the 1990s.

Above: Ducati design chief Massimo Bordi's eight-valve, liquid-cooled desmodromic powerplant brought a new level of performance and refinement to Ducati's long-standing 90-degree V-twin engine format.

Above left: The all-red 851 of 1989 had a very different style to the previous red, white and green 'tricolore' model, introducing a refined look that Ducati's eight-valve V-twins would continue in future years.

Ducati 851 (1989)

Engine	Liquid-cooled dohc eight-valve 90-degree V-twin
Capacity	851cc (92 x 64mm)
Maximum power	104bhp @ 9000rpm
Transmission	Six-speed, chain final drive
Frame	Tubular-steel ladder
Suspension	Telescopic front; single shock rear
Brakes	Twin discs front; disc rear
Weight	396lb (180kg)
Top speed	145mph (233km/h)

Index

AJS 350cc M16 52
Ariel
　　Leader 81
　　Red Hunter 350 57
　　Square Four 4G 40-41, 57
Benelli 750 Sei 124
Bimota
　　DB1 177
　　SB2 142
　　YB8 186
BMW
　　K1 188
　　K100RS 168
　　R32 22-23
　　R69S 86
　　R75 43
　　R75/5 116
　　R80 G/S 155
　　R90S 123
Bridgestone 350 GTR 95
Brough Superior 6, 32-33
BSA
　　A10 Golden Flash 61, 70
　　Gold Star DBD34 6, 58-59, 70
　　Lightning 650 111
　　Model E 21
　　Road Rocket 650 61
　　Rocket Gold Star 83
　　Spitfire MkIV 97
Buell RS1200 187
Bultaco Metralla 250 GTS 131
Crocker 29
Cyclone 17
Daimler Einspur 7
Douglas
　　2.75hp 18
　　Dragonfly 56
Dresda Triton 90-91
Ducati
　　750SS 6
　　851 7, 190-191
　　900SS 127
　　Darmah SD 149
　　Pantah 600 162
　　Scrambler 350 119
Excelsior
　　Manxman 30

Super X 20
Flying Merkel 16
FN Four 7, 10-11
Geneva 6
Gilera Saturno 47
Harley-Davidson
　　Duo-Glide 67, 88
　　Electra Glide 88, 110
　　FXST Softail 172
　　FX Super Glide 110
　　Model 11F 15
　　Model 61E 29, 31
　　Sportster 62, 110
　　V-twin 7, 15
　　WL45 46
　　XLCR1000 Café Racer 140
　　XLH 1200 Sportster 140, 183
Henderson Model KJ 26
Hesketh V1000 161
Hildebrand & Wolfmüller 1489cc 6
Honda
　　C71 69
　　CB1100R 160, 170
　　CB400F 130
　　CB450 89
　　CB72 82, 89
　　CB750 7, 106-107
　　CB900F 150, 160
　　CB92 76
　　CBR600F 181, 182
　　CBX1000 146-147
　　CX500 Turbo 164-165
　　GL1000 Gold Wing 128-129
　　RC30 184-185
　　VF1000R 170
　　VFR750F 178, 185
Indian
　　Chief 6, 50-51
　　Four 35
　　Powerplus 19, 27, 50
　　Scout 27, 50
Kawasaki
　　250SG 94
　　GPz1100 157, 171
　　GPZ900R 167, 171, 180
　　H2 750 113
　　W2TT Commander 100

Z1 120-121, 139
Z1100R 167
Z1300 144, 151
ZXR750 189
Laverda
　　750 SFC 112
　　Jota 1000 134
　　Montjuic Mk2 163
Matchless
　　G12 71
　　Model X 33
Moto Guzzi
　　Airone 7, 48
　　Falcone 77
　　Le Mans 850 136-137
　　V1000 Convert 156
　　V7 Special 102
　　V7 Sport 117
Moto Rumi 125 Sport 53
MV Agusta
　　750 Sport 122
　　Magni 143
Ner-a-Car 24
Norton
　　650SS Dominator 80
　　Big Four 34
　　Classic 182
　　Commando 98-99
　　Commando 750S 109
　　CS1 25
　　Dominator 88 49, 68, 70
　　Model 7 49, 68
Panther Model 100 73
Pierce Four 12
Pope V-twin 13
Quasar 144
Royal Enfield
　　Constellation 66
　　Continental GT 87
Rudge Ulster 28
Scott Flying Squirrel 42
Sunbeam
　　S7 De Luxe 43, 60
　　S8 60
Suzuki
　　GS1000 145, 154
　　GS750 139, 145

GSX1100 154, 166
GSX1100S Katana 166
GSX-R1100 179
GSX-R750 174-175, 176, 179
GT550 133
GT750 114-115, 126, 133
RE-5 126
T20 Super Six 93, 96
T500 96
Thomas 6
Triumph
　　Bonneville T120 7, 70, 78-79
　　Speed Twin 36-37
　　T140 Bonneville Silver Jubilee 138
　　T150 Trident 101, 118, 125
　　T160 Trident 125
　　Thunderbird 650 64-65
　　Tiger 100 37, 54
　　TR6 Trophy 72
　　X-75 Hurricane 118
Velocette
　　LE 63, 92
　　MAC 55
　　Venom Thruxton 92
Vincent
　　Rapide 44-45, 161
Yamaha
　　FJ1200 180
　　FZ750 176
　　RD350LC 158-159
　　RD400C 135
　　RD500LC 169
　　V-Max 173
　　XS-1 103
　　XS1100 148
　　XS750 141
　　XT500 132
　　YDS-2 84-85
　　YR-5 108
Zenith Gradua 14